PREHISTORIC WORLD CULTURES

First Edition

By Renee B. Walker

State University of New York, College at Oneonta

Bassim Hamadeh, CEO and Publisher
Michael Simpson, Vice President of Acquisitions
Jamie Giganti, Managing Editor
Jess Busch, Graphic Design Supervisor
John Remington, Acquisitions Editor
Brian Fahey, Licensing Associate

Copyright © 2014 by Cognella, Inc. All rights reserved. No part of this publication may be reprinted, reproduced, transmitted, or utilized in any form or by any electronic, mechanical, or other means, now known or hereafter invented, including photocopying, microfilming, and recording, or in any information retrieval system without the written permission of Cognella, Inc.

First published in the United States of America in 2014 by Cognella, Inc.

Trademark Notice: Product or corporate names may be trademarks or registered trademarks, and are used only for identification and explanation without intent to infringe.

Cover image copyright © 2013 by Depositphotos / Vaclav Volrab

Printed in the United States of America

ISBN: 978-1-62131-948-1 (pbk)/ 978-1-62131-949-8 (br)

www.cognella.com   800-200-3908

CONTENTS

List of figures	v
Introduction	1
1: Studying Past Cultures	5
2: Our Earliest Ancestors	15
3: Early Humans	23
4: Human Expansion	33
5: Transition to Food Producers	43
6: Early Agricultural Societies	51
7: Mesopotamia	61
8: North Africa	69
9: The Mediterranean	77
10: East Asia	85
11: South Asia	93
12: North America	99
13: Mesoamerica	109
14: South America	119
References Cited	127
Image Credits	133
Index	137

LIST OF FIGURES

1-1.	Image of Edward B. Tylor (Image by Beao).	5
1-2.	Horse Painting from Lascaux Cave, France dating to around 17,000 years ago.	6
1-3.	French Prehistorian Jacques Tixier teaches a student how to flintknap (Image by Jose-Manuel Benito Alvarez).	9
2-1.	Map of Africa with locations of key hominini fossils.	16
2-2.	Skull of *Sahelanthropus tchadensis* (Image by Didier Descouens)	16
2-3.	*Australopithecus afarensis* skeleton known as "Lucy."	17
2-4.	Skull of *Paranthropus boisei* (Image by Durova).	18
2-5.	Oldowan Pebble Chopper (Image by Didier Descouens).	19
2-6.	*Homo erectus* specimen known as "Turkana Boy" (Image by Claire Houck).	20
2-7.	Acheulean Tools from Kent, U.K.	21
3-1.	A map of Eurasia showing the location of ice sheets during the Pleistocene epoch.	23
3-2.	Skull of *Homo neanderthalensis* (30,000–50,000 years old) (Image by Anagoria).	24
3-3.	Levallois Core.	25
3-4.	Neanderthal burial at Kebara Cave, Israel	26
3-5.	Skuhl V skull from Qafzeh Cave, Israel (Image by Wapondaponda).	28
3-6.	Male Cro-Magnon skull from Bichon Cave, Switzerland (Image by Latenium).	28
3-7.	An atlatl (spear thrower).	29

3-8.	Venus of Willendorf (Image by Mathias Kabel).	29
3-9.	Image of extinct Elk stag (Megaloceros) with abstract design.	30
3-10.	Human and Bird in shaft panel (Image by Peter80).	31
4-1.	Map of the Sahul and Sunda landmasses (Image by Maximilian Dörrbecker).	34
4-2.	Skull from Peru showing cranial deformation (Image by Didier Descouens).	34
4-3.	Rock art from Namadgi National Park, Australia (Image by Martyman at English Language Wikipedia).	35
4-4.	Map of North America showing the extent of ice sheets during the Pleistocene epoch	36
4-5.	Example of a Clovis Point.	37
4-6.	Example of a Solutrean point.	38
4-7.	Mastodon reconstruction.	39
5-1.	Gray Wolves.	43
5-2.	A Chihuahua (Image by Tyke).	44
5-3.	Dog burial from Dust Cave, Alabama (modified from Walker et al. 2005).	46
5-4.	Pazyryk horseman.	47
5-5.	Mummy of the "Siberian Ice Maiden".	48
6-1.	Map of the Fertile Crescent (Image by Nafsadh).	51
6-2.	House foundations at Jericho.	52
6-3.	Interior house reconstruction at Çatalhöyük featuring bull heads (Image by Georges Jansoone).	53
6-4.	Red deer antler and skull headdress from Star Carr.	54
6-5.	Map of Neolithic cultures in Europe.	55
6-6.	Remains of a house structure at Skara Brae, Scotland (Image by John Burka).	55
6-7.	West Kennet Long Barrow.	56
6-8.	Stonehenge as seen today.	57
7-1.	Map of Mesopotamia that also shows current boundaries.	61
7-2.	Close up of a cuneiform tablet (Image by Matt Neale).	62
7-3.	Gold headdress buried with Queen Puabi in the Royal Tombs of Ur	62

LIST OF FIGURES | VII

7-4.	Ziggurat of Ur (Image by Hardnfast).	63
7-5.	Bronze head attributed to Sargon, but it could also be his grandson, Naram-Sin.	63
7-6.	Code of Hammurabi, the code is written in cuneiform and King Hammurabi is seated at the top.	64
7-7.	A Middle Eastern Tell (Image by Gugganji).	65
7-8.	Winged Colossal Statues from Nimrud (Image by Mujtaba Chohan).	65
7-9.	Close-up of Sculpture from Nimrud depicting Ashurnasirpal II hunting lions (Image by Ealdgyth).	66
8-1.	Map of North Africa showing the Egyptian civilization and ancient and modern cities.	69
8-2.	The Rosetta Stone (Image by Hans Hellewaert).	70
8-3.	The Narmer Tablet.	71
8-4.	The Great Pyramid, built for the Pharaoh Khufu.	72
8-5.	The gold and lapis lazuli funerary mask of Pharaoh Tutankamun.	73
9-1.	Map of the Mediterranean region with some ancient sites indicated.	77
9-2.	Frescos in a room at Knossos (Image by Chris 73/Wikimedia Commons).	78
9-3.	Bull jumping fresco at Knossos.	78
9-4.	The Phaistos Disc (Image by Aserakov).	79
9-5.	Minoan Goddess Vessel (Image by Chris 73/Wikimedia Commons).	79
9-6.	The Lions Gate at Mycenae (Image by David Monniaux).	80
10-1.	Map of East Asia.	85
10-2.	Jōmon pottery vessel.	86
10-3.	Shang Dynasty oracle bone.	87
10-4.	The tomb of Shi Huang featuring the Terra Cotta Army.	88
10-5.	Closeup of the Terra Cotta Soldiers (Image by Tomasz Sienicki).	88
10-6.	Ming vase.	89
11-1.	Map of the Indus Valley with important sites indicated.	93
11-2.	Indus Valley seals (Image by World Imaging).	94
11-3.	Great Bath at Mohenjo-daro (Image by Grjatoi).	95
11-4.	Dancing girl of Mohenjo-daro.	96

12-1.	Mound A at Poverty Point (Image by Kneimla).	100
12-2.	Map of the eastern United States showing the locations of some key mound building sites	101
12-3.	Mica hand from the Hopewell Mound Group.	102
12-4.	Monk's Mound, Cahokia (Image by QuartierLatin1968).	103
12-5.	Map of the southwestern United States showing the Four Corners area.	104
12-6.	Cliff Palace, Mesa Verde National Park (Image by Staplegunther at en.wikipedia).	105
13-1.	Map of Mesoamerica showing ancient sites and modern cities.	109
13-2.	Colossal Stone Head Monument at San Lorenzo.	110
13-3.	Pyramid of the Sun, Teotihuacan, Mexico.	111
13-4.	Temple I, Tikal, Guatemala (Image by Raymond Ostertag).	112
13-5.	El Casitllo, Chichen Itza, at the spring equinox.	113
13-6.	Reconstruction of the Tenochtitlan.	114
14-1.	Map of western South America showing some prehistoric sites.	119
14-2.	The "Monkey," a Nazca line drawing.	120
14-3.	A View of Machu Picchu, Peru (Image by Charles J.Sharp).	122
14-4.	An Incan quipu.	122

INTRODUCTION

This book is meant to complement a course in World Prehistory or Ancient World Cultures. The main focus is a broad overview of World Prehistory, while highlighting some significant events, developments, and cultures. The intention is to provide students with an understanding of changes through time, from the evolution of our species to the development of complex civilizations. Students will have a greater appreciation for human history and the accomplishments of humanity.

The book is organized mainly chronologically and geographically, though there is some overlap. Chapter One focuses on how archaeologists study past cultures. Studying past cultures can be challenging, because, unlike other social sciences, the subjects of archaeological studies are long gone and have left behind only material items that were a part of their lives. Often the materials are "garbage" (things used, broken, and discarded) and the challenge for the archaeologist is to sort through the debris to determine what was important to a group of people and reconstruct their life ways from this material. Archaeology and the study of past cultures are founded in the field of Anthropology, so the concepts of Anthropology are applied to archaeological cultures. In addition, this chapter presents some very basic information on archaeological methods, so students have an understanding of techniques employed to find, excavate, and date archaeological sites.

Chapters two through four are centered on the evolution of humans. While there are still many questions about when, where, and how we evolved, there is evidence that suggests we evolved in Africa over 6 million years ago from a species that was ancestral to chimpanzees. Chapter Two examines the earliest species that "split" from early primates. Chapter Three looks into later pre-human species, in particular Neanderthals and early *Homo sapiens* (modern humans). Chapter Four presents the spread of modern humans throughout the rest of the Asia, Australia, and Europe and the Americas.

Chapter Five delves into the beginnings of agriculture, a cultural innovation that evolved independently in many different parts of the world. The focus in this chapter is on what the transition meant for people who began to control the production of their food. It was an innovation that changed a subsistence focused on hunting and gathering and mobile living that had been a part of human life for over six million years. The Fertile Crescent, located in what is now Egypt, Jordan, Syria, and Iraq, is the earliest region for which we have evidence of plant domestication. Chapter Six continues the theme of understanding food production and changes in society by investigating increasing cultural complexity at sites such as Stonehenge, in Great Britain. This chapter also explores agricultural societies in the Middle East.

Chapter Seven's topic is Mesopotamia, which is one of the world's earliest complex societies. Complex societies are defined as having large population centers, agriculture, monumental architecture, and a writing system. The city of Uruk, located on the Euphrates River in modern Iraq, is one of the world's first cities. Uruk was part of the Sumerian civilization. Other Mesopotamian cultures are explored, including the Akkadian, Babylonian and Assyrian Empires.

In Chapter Eight we examine the region of North Africa and, specifically, the development of the early city-states of the Nile River Valley. These city-states subsequently became the Egyptian Empire. The Egyptian Empire is famous for its monumental architecture and elaborate burial ceremonies. This chapter focuses on some the influential dynasties and the accomplishments of the Egyptian Empire over time.

Chapter Nine explores the Mediterranean region. The Minoan society on the Greek island of Crete developed expansive trade networks and built at least four large palace complexes. Minoans had agriculture based on growing wheat, grapes and olives. They also developed extensive trade networks throughout the Mediterranean. The Mycenaen civilization evolved on mainland Greece and eventually became very powerful and conquered most of Greece and the Greek Islands. Finally, the Etruscan civilization evolved in western Italy and had many "Mediterranean-like" traits, such as a reliance on trade and shipping, agriculture based on wheat, wine and olives, and elaborate art and pottery.

Chapter Ten examines the early cultures of East Asia and the development of the early Japanese and Chinese civilizations. The many dynasties of the Chinese Empire had important innovations, such as the development of a monetary system, roads and canals for transporting goods, and systematized language and legislation. Also, the famous "first emperor" of China, Shi Huang, and his elaborate tomb surrounded by the Terra Cotta Soldiers is explored in this chapter.

Chapter Eleven explores South Asia and civilizations of the Indus Valley. One of the earliest is the Harappan civilization. The two largest cities of this civilization are Harappa and Mohenjo-daro. The cities are famous for being well planned and laid out, with a sewage system, baths, and mud-brick construction. Numerous artifacts, including bronze and stone sculptures, were excavated from the sites. Also, the coastal city of Lothal was important for the trade networks of the Indus Valley.

Chapter Twelve focuses on North America and the development of agriculture and sedentism in some parts of the continent. People arrived in this region during the last Ice Age and were hunters and gatherers. Eventually, during the Woodland period, agriculture was developed and populations increased. A culture known as the Mississippian spread throughout the Midwest and Southeastern United States. The Mississippian people grew corn, beans, and squash and built large flat-topped mounds and buried their dead in conical mounds. Another North America area that is explored is the Southwestern culture area. Cultures such as the Hohokam, Anasazi and Mogollon from this region are discussed. They are best known for their agricultural communities with advanced irrigation systems, kivas, cliff dwellings, and painted pottery.

Chapter Thirteen examines Mesoamerican cultures with a focus on the Maya and Aztec. The Maya are a group of city-states from southern Mexico, Belize, Guatemala, and Honduras. The Maya had elaborate trade networks and each city-state was independent with its own ruling class, priests, and armies. The Aztec Empire came into power in Northern Mexico and built an elaborate city where modern Mexico City is today. The Aztecs were known for human sacrifice and a drive to expand their empire through warfare.

Chapter Fourteen explores South America and the development of civilizations in the Andes region. Agriculture in South America developed around 6,000 years ago and later complex cultures developed elaborate trade networks and built cities with monumental architecture. Some early complex cultures in South America include the Huari, Chimu, Moche, and Nazca. In the highland region of Peru, a civilization known as the Inca conquered much of western South America and expanded the empire north to Ecuador and south to Chile.

It is hoped that this book will provide students with an overview of the world and where and when significant changes took place. The earliest origins of humans, the development of agriculture, and increasing cultural complexity are all important parts of our collective human history. It is important for students to be well-versed in world history so that they can better contextualize current news and events from around the world. Also, students can more fully appreciate the amazing innovations and accomplishments of human society by understanding what has occurred over time.

1: STUDYING PAST CULTURES

1.1 WHAT IS CULTURE?

Defining the term "culture" is very difficult to do, because there are many, broad ways it can be defined. If you asked ten of your fellow students what a "culture" is, you would probably get ten different answers. A traditional definition, put forth by anthropologist Edward B. Tylor, states it is "that complex whole which includes knowledge, belief, art, law, morals, custom, and any other capabilities and habits acquired by man as a member of society" (1871:1). You might notice that this definition of Tylor's is different from your own and you might include more categories, such as culture is a shared behavior or a system of beliefs (Figure 1-1). Anthropologists who focus on the biological aspect of humans (biological anthropologists) might define it as a non-biological means of adaptation to an environment (Relethford, 2009). That is, we use things that we make to help us live in places or conditions that would be impossible to do so otherwise. For example, we have warm clothing, structures, and a means of heat to live in very cold climates.

Another way to understand culture is to pose the question: Do non-human animals have culture? In some cases, the answer is easy. In other cases it is harder. For example, other primates, such as chimpanzees and gorillas, are very closely related to us genetically. In fact, we share 98.7% of our DNA with chimpanzees (Prufer et al., 2012). Research by Jane Goodall has shown that chimpanzees pass on information about their world to their children, that they can learn new techniques for obtaining food, such as pounding open nuts with rocks, and that different chimpanzee groups hunt in different ways (Goodall, 1969, 1986). Similarly, our parents taught us how to behave in our world, we learn how to innovate and change to make our lives better, and different groups of humans behave in different ways. Probably the most compelling information to suggest that chimpanzees have cultures is that

Figure 1-1. Image of Edward B. Tylor (Image by Beao).

chimpanzees (and gorillas) have learned to use American Sign Language and computers to communicate. Washoe, the most famous of these signing chimpanzees, learned over 350 signs and taught her adopted son many of these signs. Does the information on chimpanzees change your perception of what culture is, or do you think that only humans can have culture? I am sure that is something that each of us will have our own opinions about.

One of the reasons anthropologists are so concerned with how to define culture is that it is a field of study that emphasizes holism. Holism is centered on the concept that all parts of a culture should be studied to understand the complex whole. This term was first applied by Jan Smuts in *Holism and Evolution* as the tendency through evolution to form wholes that are greater than the sum of the parts (1973). Thus, studying one aspect of a culture necessitates understanding all aspects of it. For example, if an archaeologist is interested in how people get food, they need to also understand how the society is organized, what the environment is like where they live, what beliefs they might have, and what their technology is, because all of these things are inter-related with subsistence.

In order to apply the concept of holism, researchers who study the past need to understand some assumptions about culture. The first is that culture is learned (Kottak, 2011). While there are some things that we come into the world knowing how to do instinctively (such as getting nourishment or crying to get the attention of our parents), there are many things we do not know. So, we learn these things from our parents mainly by their communicating to us how to behave within our culture. Can you think of things you learned from your parents or family at a young age that helped shape your lives? You probably learned how to eat with a spoon, how to behave in public, and how to speak a language, to name a very few. It is the same with all cultures, past and present.

Culture is also based on symbols (Kottak, 2011). Symbols are an essential part of culture and we use them all the time to communicate. A symbol is something verbal or nonverbal within a culture that comes to stand for something else. Language is one of the most important symbols and the main way culture is transmitted from one person to another. We usually learn one main language, but many families are bi-lingual or multi-lingual. Babies typically say their first word between eleven and fourteen months, but they absorb language from the moment they are born. First, babies learn by imitation, and then they start putting their own ideas and thoughts into words. We also learn to recognize other symbols that are common in our world. In American culture, for example, we learn to recognize street signs, signs around the house, and signs at school. Signs and languages of the past can be more difficult to interpret. Some cultures did not record their language in writing and even if they did, they might be difficult to decipher completely. Also, many signs are specific to a particular culture. An example would be the cave art of the Upper Paleolithic era (Figure 1-2). These cave drawings of animals and abstract shapes have been studied for many years, but can we truly understand all the meaning these images had for Upper Paleolithic people? Probably not all of it, but we can apply the techniques of holism to understand the context of them.

Figure 1-2. Horse Painting from Lascaux Cave, France dating to around 17,000 years ago.

Culture is shared between members of a particular group (Kottak, 2011). The sharing of culture is what unifies a group and gives them a common identity. The sharing can take the form of a common language, common religion, or common lifestyles. In some cases, culture can be broadly shared. For example, people might identify themselves as part of an "American" culture or they might identify themselves as a "New Englander." It could also be defined more narrowly, so someone might identify with a college, a town, or a neighborhood. What makes a shared culture is that there are aspects within that group that are specific only to them. A past culture might have a stone tool manufacturing technique, a design on pottery, or a clothing style that is unique to them. For example, when someone sees a steep-sided pyramid made out of stone, the usual reaction is that it is an "Egyptian" pyramid. It is not a universal that all ancient Egyptians were buried in pyramids, because it was reserved for royals, but it is a visual commonality that identifies a culture in time and space.

Another aspect of culture is that it is integrated (Kottak, 2011). This relates directly back to the concept in holism, in that if one aspect of culture is changed, it tends to affect other parts of a culture. One big example is the beginnings of agriculture in various cultures. We will talk about this in detail later, but it was a huge change for cultures that previously hunted for and gathered their food. Agriculturalists are more tethered to the land, because they need to tend to their crops. They built permanent settlements, the population expanded, and social structure became more complex. All of these changes occurred from a change in how people produce their food. We will be learning a lot about how both large and small changes can alter cultures.

Culture is also adaptive. As discussed previously, humans are the main species that uses culture to adapt to their environment. It is a large part of why we have migrated from Africa to live on every continent in the world. We discovered how to make stone tools from materials in our environment, harness fire, make clothing, and construct shelters to adapt to different habitats. Certainly animals do this, but no other species has been able to adapt to so many different environments. Our ability to adapt and change has made us one of the most powerful organisms on our planet. The means of adaptation and changes in how we adapt is a major factor of this text.

Finally, culture is dynamic. Culture changes all the time. In the distant past, these changes were much more gradual. For example, some cultures stayed the same for hundreds of thousands of years. In these cases we see only small changes in culture due to changes in environment or population levels. In the more recent past, these changes accelerate and we see alterations in behavior that can be seen in thousands or hundreds of years. Abrupt changes can also infrequently occur and these are often related to catastrophic environmental changes or events such as warfare. The tempo and frequency of these changes is something that archaeologists are interested in identifying, as well as the reasons behind the changes.

In addition to using the assumptions of culture to help understand past cultures, Anthropologists also use the concept of cultural relativism. Cultural relativism is when a person does not judge a culture by their own culture's norms (Kottak, 2011). This sounds like an easy thing to do, but it is really difficult. We will learn that some cultures practiced human sacrifice, which is something that is very hard to understand. Also, it is complicated to put aside the norms of our own culture to look objectively at another. I like to think of it as putting on my "cultural relativity" hat when I start to get judgmental about another group—whether past or present.

There are also some universals of culture, which are features found in every society. They might also be called fundamentals of culture. These include, but are not limited to, art, bodily adornment, cooking, education, family, incest taboos, language, and music. There are variations in some of these things. For example, not all cultures identify incest taboos the same way. Many of the royal families of Egypt and the Aztec married very closely within their families to keep the blood lines pure, so we often see half-sisters and -brothers marrying within the dynasties. Also, you might notice that agriculture is not on the list above. Not all cultures adopted agriculture as a subsistence strategy. Some groups, such as the Plains Indians of North America, hunted and traded until the arrival of Europeans. They had a very complex social system that persisted for over ten thousand years. So, you might want to think about some cultural universals that are not mentioned above.

I have mentioned that much about what anthropologists study is how cultures change, which is related to the dynamic nature of culture. The main ways cultures change is by invention, diffusion, and migration. An example of culture change through invention is the control of fire. It may be that it was an accident—lightning may have struck a tree and the fire was kept going through human intervention. Or rocks could have been struck together to cause a spark in dry grass. Either way, it was a huge change for our ancestors. They would have light at night, heat, and a way to cook their food. Culture can also change through diffusion. This is when two cultures that live near each other come into contact and share ideas and technology. Culture can also change through migration, which is when groups travel long distances and then come into contact with each other. This often constitutes large changes, such as when Europeans arrived in the Americas and brought iron technology, such as guns, and horses.

Changes that are often tracked in the evolution of cultures are those of social organization. Social organizations of prehistoric cultures are broadly grouped into bands, tribes, chiefdoms, city-states, and empires. Your first thought on seeing the term "bands" in the above list probably had to do with music, but a band is a social organization that is typically associated with people who hunt for and gather their food and have relatively small groups. The groups usually number 30 to 50 people, but this can vary from year to year and at certain times of the year (Kottak, 2011). Bands are also typically not sedentary, but move around from place to place depending on where food resources might be located at a given time. They are usually egalitarian (all members have equal access to wealth, power, and prestige) and have no formal leadership. Bands of hunter-gatherers were found throughout the world in many different environments until very recently. Today, no bands live exclusively by hunting and gathering and generally trade with neighbors for agriculture products. Also, traditional band territories have been drastically reduced. In the past, however, all humans lived in band-level societies as hunters and gatherers until approximately 10,000 years ago when agriculture was developed in some parts of the world.

Tribes are larger than bands and have a slightly more formal leadership institution with a chief or "big man" who leads the group. The leadership position is not usually hereditary and leaders are usually chosen by their personal abilities, rather than what family they are born into. Tribes are also typically either horticulturalists (cultivate family gardens) or pastoralists (herd domestic animals). Tribes can be sedentary or semi-sedentary, with horticulturalists usually sedentary or moving only every few years and those tribes with a pastoral economy moving seasonally with the herds or sometimes a small number of people will move with the herd, while the majority of the group (mostly women and children) live in one village year round.

Chiefdoms, like bands and tribes, are generally based on family ties. The difference with a chiefdom is that different families, age and gender groups have different statuses. Also, leadership tends to be hereditary with chiefdoms, so that leaders (usually male) are chosen from one family line. Thus, all members of that line generally enjoy higher status than other families in the chiefdom. Chiefdoms also have a very broad range of members that can vary depending on resources and tensions within in the group. For example, if tensions are high within a particular family or group of families, they may fission off and form a new chiefdom in an adjacent area. Chiefdoms are usually associated with agriculture as a food resource, but some chiefdoms have developed in groups that are still hunters and gatherers, but this usually occurs only with groups that rely on fishing for subsistence. Chiefdoms are also sedentary with much larger villages than tribes.

A city-state is a social organization that has a large urban center and outlying territories under the control of one government. This government is typically a monarchy where the leader is chosen from one family and that person's leadership controls the government. City-states also share common language, religion, and subsistence. One example of a city-state social organization that we will talk about later in the book is the Maya. The Maya thrived in Mesoamerica, which is today southern Mexico, Belize, Guatemala, and Honduras. There were many Maya cities, but each one was autonomous, with their own king and royal family, priests, officials, armies, merchants, and farmers. These cities had smaller villages and towns that came under their rule. However, while each city was autonomous, all the Mayan cities shared common language, religion, agriculture, and trade.

An empire is a large geographic area that is ruled by one monarch or ruling family. Often, there is one capital city where the monarch lives, but there are many cities, villages, and towns within the empire. The people who are included in the empire may be distinct from the rulers and may have been forced to become part of the empire through warfare. The Egyptian Empire is one example. The city-states along the Nile River were conquered and unified by Narmer 5,000 years ago and he declared himself the first Pharaoh, which was technically the beginning of the Egyptian Empire. The Egyptian Empire spread to encompass territories in Africa and the Middle East and lasted for over 2,800 years. An empire may have an "official" language and religion, but there may be multiple languages, religions, and subsistence practices represented.

1.2 BASIC CONCEPTS IN ARCHAEOLOGY

There are four main goals that archaeologists attempt to accomplish when studying the past. The first is to gain an understanding of culture history for the areas they study. A culture history is a timeline that documents changes for a region, on both broad and narrow scales. These timelines are developed to show changes in cultures over periods of time, usually based on technological changes or socio-cultural changes. One major change in the Americas is the domestication of plants. This occurred in the northeastern and southeastern regions between 5,000 and 3,000 years ago, with many people relying predominantly on agriculture by 3,000 years ago, so this would be an important part of the culture history of prehistoric eastern North America. These timelines help archaeologist studying in these regions compare their research. For example, an archaeologist working on a site dating to around 4,000 years ago in New York might be talking to an archaeologist working on site dating to around the same time in Alabama. They would know that each of them probably have sites where people are mostly hunters and gatherers, have not yet developed pottery, and live in non-sedentary settlements. Once this is established, they can go into more detail on what differences there are between the groups and what might be causing those differences.

Another goal is reconstructing past life ways. Archaeologists might try to replicate technologies or practices of the past to better understand how people lived. One technology that has been studied quite a bit is the manufacturing of stone tools. This is a process known as flintknapping, where a piece of flint or chert (material that is most often used to make stone tools) is struck by another object (usually a stone or antler hammer) to flake off pieces of the original piece to create a stone tool (Figure 1-3). We can learn a lot about what went into making a stone tool in the past by learning about this process. For example, we can find out about where they would go to get the raw material to make their stone tools. Also, we can learn what steps they went through to make the tools. Finally, we are better able to understand how they used the tools by observing how the tools cut, chop, or scrape different materials such as meat, wood, and hides.

A third goal of archaeology is to explain culture change. We discussed previously that change usually occurs through invention, diffusion, and migration. It can sometimes be hard to pinpoint exactly how and when a culture changed, particularly when that change is slow and gradual. These changes, like the adoption of agriculture, might also take place because of multiple issues. We will discuss in a later chapter that some researchers think agriculture began because of environmental change, some think it was due to increasing population size, and others believe it was both changes working together.

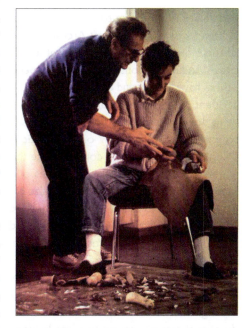

Figure 1-3. French Prehistorian Jacques Tixier teaches a student how to flintknap (Image by Jose-Manuel Benito Alvarez).

Other changes are more abrupt, particularly when two cultures come into contact and a culture changes technology because of this contact. An example here would be the adoption of metal tools by Native Americans after Europeans arrive, particularly metal cooking pots, knives, and guns. It is often with explaining culture change that the holistic point of view is applied, because changes generally occur for many reasons. It is important to look at all factors, including environmental and cultural, to see how change comes about.

Finally, archaeologists also work to make the past relevant to the present. While much of archaeology can be esoteric and information gained through archaeological research not applicable to the modern world, many things can be of interest in recent times. One area in particular is the study of disease. Many diseases have been around for a very long time and this field of study is known as paleopathology. The field of paleopathology works to understand the history of disease and then uses this to predict what may happen to the disease and the populations it affects in the future. Tuberculosis, for example, has been a problem for humanity for a very long time (Roberts, 1995). Tuberculosis is first seen almost 8,000 years ago in Africa and the Middle East when people began to domesticate cattle. When humans consume meat and milk that are contaminated with tuberculosis bacteria, they can become infected and then transmit the disease to other humans (Jansens, 1970; Roberts, 1995). The disease manifests itself in the human skeleton in advanced form through damage of the joints of the body and can also be found through DNA extracted from the bone.

Thus, the four main goals of archaeology are to study culture history, reconstruct past life ways, study culture change, and make archaeology relevant to the present.

1.3 SURVEY AND EXCAVATION TECHNIQUES

People are often drawn to archaeology because it seems like an exciting adventure, thanks to movies featuring Indiana Jones and Lara Croft. Archaeology can be fun and exciting, but there is also a lot of work involved. One of the most frequent questions I get asked when I tell people that I am an archaeologist is, "how do you find sites?" And my response is always, "it depends." Some sites are found through systematic survey and testing, while others have been found completely by accident. Some of the most famous sites in the world have been found by accident, such as the cave art site of Lascaux, France, which was found by four young men in 1940 when their dog went down a hole in the French countryside (Bahn, 2007). We cannot always count on finding sites by accident, so we usually have to rely on systematic surveys. The scope of the survey will depend on why the survey is being conducted. In some countries, like the United States, there are federal laws requiring a survey for cultural materials if there are public properties or public funds involved in construction or other public works. In this case, the survey is constricted by the size of the construction project. For example, if a highway is being increased from two lanes to four, a survey will need to be done along the corridor of the new boundaries. If materials are found, the highway route might be changed or the artifacts excavated for further research. An archaeological project that is funded by research grants from institutions such as the National Science Foundation may have more leeway when designing the survey.

Whatever the reason for the survey, there are certain methods applied to maximize the possibility of finding archaeological remains. A surface survey can be done if the soil is visible (a recently plowed field, for example). If the ground surface is not visible, then subsurface testing needs to be conducted. The most basic of these is to dig shovel test pits across the area being investigated. The shovel tests vary in size from 30–50 centimeters in diameter and can be over a meter deep. The interval for placing the tests can be ten meters apart, but will vary depending on the project. A more technologically complex method is to use remote-sensing equipment to "see" through the sediment and detect any anomalies that might be of archaeological significance. One remote-sensing technique is ground-penetrating radar. This machine sends an electromagnetic pulse down through the sediment and will reflect back any subsurface features. The area where the features are found can then be concentrated on for archaeological testing and excavations. Often, both subsurface shovel tests and remote-sensing devices are employed to locate potential sites.

The second most frequent question I get when talking about my job is, "how do you excavate?" Again, the answer is, "it depends." One of the most interesting things about archaeology is that each site is unique. You might excavate with a brush, a spoon, a trowel, or a shovel depending on what you find and where the site is located. Many people are surprised that we also sometimes excavate with heavy equipment, such as backhoes. Backhoes can be used when a survey has found that a site is deeply buried by layers of soil that contain no artifacts (what we would call sterile levels). A lot of time can be saved if the sterile material is removed with heavy equipment; then more time can be spent excavating the archaeological levels by hand.

The size of the area excavated will depend on what was found in the survey. Some sites can cover many acres, whereas others are only several meters in area. If a site is very large, but not very deep, a horizontal excavation technique where a wider area is excavated is often used. If a site is very deep, such as in cave deposits, a vertical excavation technique may be used, where a trench or narrow area is excavated to greater depths. Regardless of the size of the site, the excavation area is laid out on a grid with north, south, east, and west coordinates for each unit. A unit is the basic area of excavation and the size of the unit will be decided based on the goals of the project. Most excavation units are about one to two meters square. A level is the depth that is excavated in each unit. These can be arbitrary levels, cultural levels, or natural levels. An arbitrary level is when the excavators dig to a set depth, such as five or ten centimeters down for each level. So, level one would be from 0–5 centimeters, level two from 5–10 centimeters, and so on. The archaeologists might also determine that they want to excavate any cultural or natural stratum (a layer of soil with similar characteristics) separately. Thus, they could excavate cultural stratum one and it would be to whatever depth that corresponds to the cultural deposits. Sometimes all three techniques are combined, which is something that I have frequently done in excavations.

All the sediment excavated from the units should be screened for archaeological materials. Screens are usually wooden frames with wire mesh for sifting dirt to find materials. The size of the holes in the wire mesh determines how big the materials are, so using a finer mesh is usually the best approach to find small pieces of stone tools or animal bones from a site. Finding plant remains, however, usually requires a more advanced technique called flotation. Flotation is when the dirt from a unit is put into a container of water. The dirt is gently agitated and eventually small bits of plants, such as seeds and charcoal, float to the top of the water. These can then be skimmed off to save for future analysis. Flotation is used because the plant remains are so small and can often be crushed when the dirt is put into a sifting screen. Using flotation can be time consuming, however, so most excavators use a combined technique of sifting screens and flotation.

Whatever technique is used for excavation, it is important to take notes about how the excavation was conducted and to map all of the materials and changes in sediments found while working. I like to encourage students to pretend they are taking notes for something that nobody will read for another hundred years, so they should be as detailed as possible and not take for granted that this person knows anything about the site. Finding artifacts in place and documenting their location is also known as finding something *in situ*, which in turn, helps document the provenience of the material. Provenience is the three-dimensional location of archaeological materials at a site. This is important to document because units are excavated at different times and different paces. For long-term projects, units next to each other might get excavated years apart. The provenience is how archaeologists associate all of the materials at the site to understand what activities occurred and when these activities took place.

The materials excavated from the site can vary, but are usually placed into broad categories. The first category is artifacts. Artifacts are objects that have been modified by humans for a particular purpose. The most common of these are stone tools, which we discussed briefly in this chapter. Prehistoric people went to flint or chert quarries, obtained raw material, and then shaped them for use as projectile points (arrow- and spear-heads), axe heads, knives, etc. Pottery is another example of an artifact, in which clay is gathered from river banks, shaped and then fired to become a cooking or storage vessel. Another category is ecofacts. Ecofacts are natural materials used by humans. The best example is the charcoal found in fire pits at archaeological sites. Humans collected the wood and burned it, and then the charcoal is left behind. The charcoal can sometimes be identified to a particular type of tree to help understand the environment people were living in. Animal bones left over from meals are also examples of ecofacts. Finally, features are the non-moveable remains of human activity. A common feature is a hearth or fire pit. Typically round or oval in shape and containing rocks and high levels of charcoal, hearths have been around for over one million years. Another type of feature would be a house structure made of stone. All of the artifacts, ecofacts, and features at a site are studied to understand the context of all the materials. Context is the association of everything found at the site and all of this combined: artifacts, ecofacts, features, and their context are what make up the archaeological record.

There are materials that are used for dating archaeological sites and there are generally two ways archaeological sites are dated. One is relative dating, and the other is called absolute. Relative dating is when you have one site or object that is older or younger than another. There is no calendar date associated in this case. Often, the Law of Superposition is used to establish relative age at a site. The Law of Superposition states that layers of sediment are deposited over time, with the oldest at the bottom and the youngest at the top (Kearey, 2001). Thus, the deeper you excavate a site, the older the material. Artifacts associate with these levels can be compared to other sites as well, using seriation. Seriation is when materials from multiple sites are put into chronological order. So, Artifact A from one site is younger than Artifact B and so on.

Another dating method is called absolute dating and determines the chronologic age of artifacts or ecofacts from a site using the physical or chemical properties of that material. The most common technique is radiocarbon dating. Radiocarbon dating can be applied to any organic materials, such as bone, charcoal, shell, and plant remains (Chazan, 2011). It is based on the principle that all living things absorb carbon over time. When these organisms die, the carbon starts to decay at a known rate, which is known as the half-life. In order to apply this to archaeological materials, the organic objects are measured for the amount of carbon remaining, and then the age of the material can be calculated. Radiocarbon dating can be applied to materials dating back as far as 70,000 years ago using a method known as accelerator mass spectrometry, which measures the amount of carbon in the object at the atomic level. While some archaeologists specialize in absolute dating methods, it is important for many archaeologists to understand what material the method can be used to date, how far back the method can be applied, and how to collect the material. The other technique that will be applied widely for our purposes is Potassium-argon dating. Potassium-argon dating is most often used when determining the age of our earliest ancestors, as it can date materials over 100,000 years old. It does not determine the age of the remains themselves, but actually measures the volcanic material deposited above and below the ancestral remains (Chazan, 2011). Potassium-argon dating takes volcanic material and measures the decay of potassium into argon.

1.4 BRINGING IT TOGETHER

We have talked about a lot of different subjects in this chapter. We discussed how cultures are studied and the ways that anthropologists study past cultures. We defined culture and holism and the assumptions of culture. All of these are used to understand cultures of the past and how we can understand them better. We also explored some of the basic concepts of archaeology, such as what sites are and what do we call the objects found at sites. Also, how sites are found and excavated is an important part of studying past cultures. Dating methods help us contextualize the information and better compare the data from different kinds of sites in different parts of the world. I hope you enjoyed a little about the concepts of studying past cultures and the goals researchers are trying to accomplish.

Key Terms and Concepts

Culture	That complex whole that includes knowledge, belief, art, law, morals, custom, and any other capabilities and habits acquired by man as a member of society. Also, the non-biological means humans use to adapt to their environment.
Holism	The tendency to form wholes that are greater than the sum of the parts.
Assumptions of Culture	Culture is learned, symbolic, shared, integrated, adaptive, and dynamic.
Cultural Relativism	Evaluating other cultures without imposing our own cultural values.
Cultural Universals	Traits found in every culture.
Culture Change	Change is usually by invention, diffusion, or migration.
Social Organizations	Bands, tribes, chiefdoms, city-states, empires.
Bands	A social organization of related people, usually small (30–50 people) who hunt and gather for a living and live a nomadic life.
Tribes	A social organization with slightly more formal leadership, sedentary or semi-sedentary, and often making a living through agriculture.
Chiefdoms	A social organization also based on family relationships, but some family lines have more status than others. Leadership can often be hereditary and groups are sedentary, with agriculture and pastoralism as a way of life.
City-States	Independent cities that have their own government, armies, priests, merchants, and commoners. They have their own territories, but share a language, religion, and way of life with a broader group.
Empire	A large territory under the control of one government. The government has one monarch and the social organization and religion of that monarch is imposed on the territories that the empire controls.
Main goals of archaeology	Studying culture history, reconstructing past life ways, explaining culture change, making archaeology relevant to the present.

Survey	Techniques used to locate sites, such as surface survey, shovel test pits, ground-penetrating radar.
Excavation	Techniques used to uncover archaeological remains. A variety of techniques can be employed, including horizontal and vertical techniques.
Unit	Basic area of archaeological excavation.
Level	Depth of excavation, including arbitrary, cultural, and natural levels.
Artifact	An object that has been modified by humans for a particular use.
Ecofact	A natural material used by humans in the past.
Feature	A non-moveable remnant of human activity.
Site	An area of human activity.
Context	The relationship of materials from a site.
Provenience	Where objects are found at a site, specifically the three-dimensional location of the material.
In situ	Finding an artifact or ecofact in its original position.
Archaeological Record	All the materials from a site, including artifacts, ecofacts, and features
Screening	Finding artifacts by sifting dirt through a mesh screen.
Flotation	Putting dirt into a container of water and the ecofacts float to the surface to be screened off.
Relative Dating	Dating artifacts in relation to one another using the Law of Superposition and Seriation.
Absolute Dating	Using the chemical or physical properties of archaeological materials to obtain a calendar date for a site.
Radicarbon Dating	An absolute dating technique that measures the decay of carbon in organic remains.
Potassium-argon Dating	An absolute dating method that measures the decay of potassium into argon in volcanic materials.

2: OUR EARLIEST ANCESTORS

2.1 EARLY ANCESTORS

There are many different ideas about how humans came to be living on the planet today. Many of those ideas are religious and use religious texts and teachings to explain our origins. However, Anthropology applies the scientific method to explain the origins of humans. The scientific method argues that we evolved over a period of time through natural selection. The concept of natural selection was first published by Charles Darwin in 1859 and is used to explain how organisms evolve and adapt to changes in their environment. Scientists believe that our last shared common ancestor with the primates lived in Africa six million years ago (Relethford, 2009). Currently, our closest living non-human primate relatives are chimpanzees and we share about 98% of our DNA with modern chimpanzees. The line leading to modern humans branched off to evolve into several species over time and ultimately modern humans arose. But, what happened in the six million years during that evolutionary process?

First, we should define what is included in our category of early ancestors. The term "hominini" is used to describe modern humans and their ancestors and it is often shortened to hominin. The term "hominini" is part of the structure for describing organisms and uses evolutionary relationships to understand their associations. Using this information to determine the biologic categorization of species is applied to both living and ancestral organisms.

For the purposes of studying our human ancestors, we will be focusing on the period starting approximately six million years ago when the human lineage first arose. The hominins in this group are collectively referred to as the basal hominins (basal meaning base or earliest). It is unclear which of the following species is the "missing link." This can sometimes be frustrating for students, who often want a concrete answer, but there are huge spans of time to consider and finding fossils is a lot like finding a needle in a haystack. This is due to several factors. The first is that the skeletal material has to become incorporated in the archaeological record. This means the organism has to die and become buried without being disturbed by animals. Second, the material needs to become fossilized. Fossilization is when the organic component of the bone is leached out and replaced by the inorganic components of the surrounding soil over time. Next, it has to be recovered by archaeologists. Often there are particular areas, such as the Great Rift Valley in Africa, where deposits are exposed in the steep

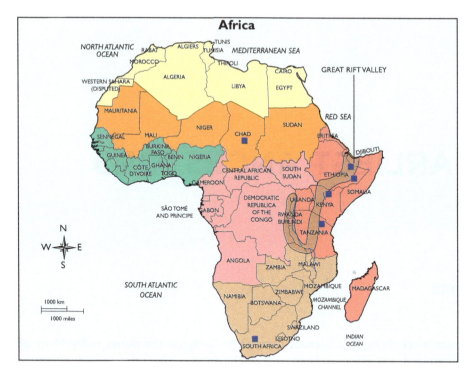

Figure 2-1. Map of Africa with locations of key hominini fossils.

rock faces of the valley. Sometimes they are found deeply buried in caves, like the caves of South Africa. It does not mean that hominins did not live throughout Africa, just that the deposition of the fossils in those areas make it more likely they will be recovered.

The basal hominins are most readily distinguished from other hominins living at that time by their tendency to walk on two legs instead of four. As we know, chimpanzees and other great apes walk on four legs, though they can occasionally be seen walking short stretches or reaching for something on two legs. Thus, our earliest ancestors must have obtained an advantage in their environment by a bipedal mode of walking. Some ideas for advantages include greater ease of movement in a mixed forest and grasslands environment, the ability to see predators with heads at a higher level (Jordania, 2011), a greater ability to obtain and carry food (Hunt, 1996; Lovejoy, 1981), and increased ability to withstand heat through upright posture, allowing more cooling and having less body area exposed to the sun (Wheeler, 1984). Whatever the explanation, it is clear that bipedality is the trait that first separated us from other organisms at that time. Determining bipedality of ancient remains can be done by looking at parts of the body that have to do with locomotion and body posture. For example, the feet, knees, pelvis, and the base of the skull can reveal if an organism was bipedal or not.

Thus, the basal hominins share at least one trait—bipedality. But, what other traits do they share? In general, they have a short stature, between three and three-and-a-half feet tall. Their brain size is about the same size as that of a chimpanzee, around 350 cubic centimeters (cm^3), which is much smaller than modern humans (with a range between 1,100 and 1,300 cm^3). They also tend to have large canines

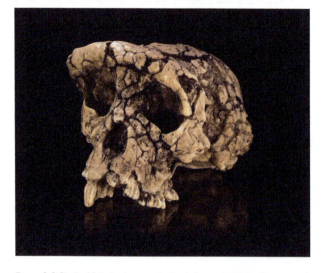

Figure 2-2. Skull of *Sahelanthropus tchadensis* (Image by Didier Descouens)

with the lower part of the face projecting outward. We do not have any evidence that they used tools or built structures and they probably lived in small groups and foraged in a way that is similar to that of modern chimpanzees.

The earliest basal hominin discovered so far is *Sahelanthropus tchadensis* (also known as the Chad skull), found in the country of Chad in 2001 (Brunet et al., 2002). It consists of one skull and the shape of the base of the skull it was bipedal (Figure 2-2). The specimen dates to over six million years ago. However, there are some problems with the specimen; only one example has been found and there are no postcranial (skeletal elements below the neck) remains associated with the skull.

The second oldest hominin is *Orrorin tugenensis*. This species was found in Kenya in 2000 and dates to six million years ago (Senut et al., 2001). Twenty elements of this species were found, including teeth, mandible, femur, humerus, and finger bones. The evidence suggests it was bipedal, but elongated arms means it may have also climbed trees. Teeth and the size of the cranium are similar to the Chad skull.

Finally, there is a basal hominin found in Ethiopia known as *Ardipithecus ramidus*. "Ardi," as the specimen was nicknamed, is that of an adult female and it is a remarkably complete specimen, considering that it dates to 4.5 million years ago (White et al., 2009). Ardi was bipedal, but had elongated arms and an opposable big toe, indicating that it was also at home in the trees. The cranial size is similar to that of the two previously mentioned basal hominins.

2.2 AUSTRALOPITHECINES AND PARANTHROPUS

After about 4 million years ago, we see a huge expansion of the number of hominins in Africa. I think this can often be confusing, because many of us have a tendency to think of evolution as a straight line or a tree limb. However, it is more likely that the evolution of our species was like a bush, with all sorts of random limbs. Some of these lines came to a dead end and some continued on to evolve and eventually become modern humans. Between four and two million years ago, it was definitely the case that there were many hominins on the landscape. The most prevalent of these was a group known as the Australopithecines. Australopithecines include several species of the genus *Australopithecus*. All of the specimens from this genus have been found in Africa, and most in East or South Africa. They also are similar in terms of the size of the teeth (slightly smaller canines than the basal hominins), the shape and size of the skull (cranial capacity around 450), and the body size (3–4 feet in height).

Australopithecus afarensis is probably the most famous of the Australopithecines, because of the completeness of a skeleton nicknamed "Lucy" (Figure 2-3). Also, it is best known because this was the first specimen where scientists identified that being bipedal was the main characteristic that differentiated early hominins from primates. Discovered in 1972 in Ethiopia, Lucy dates to around 3.2 million years ago (Johanson and Maitland, 1981).

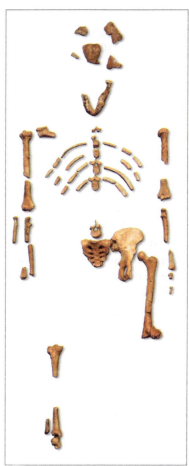

Figure 2-3. *Australopithecus afarensis* skeleton known as "Lucy."

Figure 2-4. Skull of *Paranthropus boisei* (Image by Durova).

Six years after the discovery of "Lucy," another team of researchers led by Mary Leakey found footprints preserved in volcanic ash in Tanzania. These footprints became known as the "Laetoli footprints" for the area of Africa where they were found. The prints were those of bipedal organisms with an arch in the foot and the big toe in line with the rest of the toes. Initial interpretations suggested that there were two individuals—one with a foot slightly larger than the other walking side by side in a layer of volcanic ash that had become wet from rainfall (Leakey, 1981). The volcanic ash, as we discussed in Chapter 1, can be dated using potassium-argon dating and the timeline established for the footprints is 3.6 million years ago.

Another species of Australopithecine, *Australopithecus anamensis*, was discovered by Meave Leakey and her team in Kenya in 1994 (Leakey et al., 1995). The specimens, largely consisting of crania and teeth, though one tibia fragment was found, date to around 4.2–3.9 million years ago. Another fossil species from South Africa that dates to between 3 and 2 million years ago was studied by Raymond Dart (1925). The specimen he studied, known as the Taung child, had a small cranium and the base of the skull exhibited evidence of bipedality. His observations were dismissed at the time, because in the early 20th century most scientists believed that our earliest ancestors would have large brains and be found first in Europe. However, current research supports bipedality as the first indication of humanity.

Australopithecus garhi was discovered in 1996 in Ethiopia (Asfaw et al., 1999). It dates to 2.5 million years ago and the fossils were associated with the oldest known stone tools, which we will discuss later. Other characteristics such as tooth morphology, cranial capacity, and body size are very similar to previously mentioned Australopithecines.

Living at around the same time as the Australopithecines was another group of hominins known as *Paranthropus* (Relethford, 2009). *Paranthropus* had very different characteristics from the Australopithecines; specifically, they were much more heavily built and taller (over 4 feet). They had extremely large teeth, particularly the molars, and wear on the teeth suggests they ate a diet that was hard to chew, such as tough leaves and grasses. Finally, most specimens have a crest on the top of the skull (see Figure 2-4) that suggests they had extra muscle attachment areas for greater chewing power.

There are three species of *Paranthropus*, including *P. boisei*, *P. robustus*, and *P. aethiopicus*. These specimens date between 2.5 and 1.5 million years ago. *P. boisei* and *P. aethiopicus* are found in East Africa (Tanzania and Ethiopia, respectively) and *P. robustus* is found in South Africa. Most scientists agree that the *Paranthropus* species represent a branch that went extinct around 1.5 million years ago and did not contribute directly to future evolution of humans. There are several theories regarding their extinction, but the most prevalent one is that the climate changed around 1.5 million years ago and the *Paranthropus* species were not able to evolve and adapt to these changes.

2.3 HOMO HABILIS AND HOMO ERECTUS

We now turn to two specimens that have the genus name *Homo*, which is the same as our own. Scientists believe that these specimens are on the ancestral line that eventually leads to us, because they show traits that are more "modern." These more modern traits are larger cranial capacity, taller statures, more modern-looking teeth and crania, and the ability to make and use stone tools. *Homo habilis* was the first species to exhibit these more modern traits.

Homo habilis was first identified by Mary and Louis Leakey in 1960 in Olduvai Gorge, Tanzania (Leakey et al., 1965). Subsequent examples of this species have been found throughout Africa and they date between 2.5 and 1.6 million years ago. They have a slightly more rounded cranium than the Australopithecines, with a cranial capacity between 500 and 700 cm^3. They are also taller on average than Australopithecines (over four and a half feet). In addition to the physical appearance of *H. habilis*, they are the first ancestor to have consistently used stone tools. We mentioned previously that *A. garhi* had stone tools associated with their fossils, but the numbers of artifacts associated with *H. habilis* are much greater and the use of tools is spread across many sites.

The types of stone tools associated with *H. habilis* are small pebble choppers known as the Oldowan tool industry. The onset of consistent tool use is part of the Lower Paleolithic (also known as the Early Stone Age) period. The Oldowan tools are made by flintknapping, a technique for making stone tools that we discussed briefly in Chapter 1. The first step in manufacturing stone tools is to obtain stone raw material, such as flint, chert, quartz, quartzite, basalt, or obsidian. These materials have what are known as "cryptocrystalline" properties, which means they have glass-like properties and break with a sharp edge. A hammerstone, which is usually a round stone or a shortened piece of wood or antler, is used to strike the raw material and remove small pieces known as flakes. The individual flakes can be useful for cutting, but the process is usually to remove multiple flakes to obtain a suitable cutting or chopping edge on the original piece of material (also known as a core). Thus, the Oldowan tools are characteristically smooth on one surface and sharp on another and were probably not hafted (attached to a handle) for use (Figure 2-5).

The evidence of stone tool use does not preclude the use of other types of tools. Certainly, wood and other organic material could have been useful to early hominins, but unfortunately, this rarely survives at archaeological sites, particularly sites that are very old. However, the Oldowan tools used by *H. habilis* do give us some more insight into their behavior. One question, in particular, is did these hominins hunt? There is not much evidence to suggest this at earlier hominin sites, including a lack of stone tools and animal bones, but we have both at *H. habilis* locations, suggesting that they were consuming more meat than their predecessors did. Analysis of the kinds of animal bones at these sites indicate that it is more likely *H. habilis* scavenged meat from other kills than that they actively hunted. This is because most of the animal bones found at *H. habilis* sites are from the lower limbs and other "non-meaty" elements of animals. If they were hunting animals and were first at the kill, then you would expect that the meatier parts of animals would be brought back to a safe place

Figure 2-5. Oldowan Pebble Chopper (Image by Didier Descouens).

for consumption. Thus, the Oldowan pebble choppers and flakes were probably used to break off lower leg bones from other predators' kills, rather than directly bringing down the animals themselves.

The second species to be designated with the genus *Homo* is *Homo erectus*. Oddly enough, given our focus on Africa to this point, the first *H. erectus* fossil was discovered in Java, Indonesia in 1891 by Eugene Dubois. Subsequent *H. erectus* fossils were found in Asia, the Middle East, Europe, and Africa, though the earliest fossils come from Africa. Thus, *H. erectus* was the first of our ancestors to leave Africa and spread to other parts of the world. *H. erectus* fossils date from 1.9 to 1 million years ago and have even more modern traits than *H. habilis*. In particular, *H. erectus* has a very large cranium (between 850 and 1,100 cm^3). They are also generally much taller than previous hominins, with some male specimens estimated to be over five-and-a-half feet tall. One specimen in particular, known as "Turkana Boy" (Figure 2-6), was found at Nairokotome near Lake Turkana, Kenya and might have been as tall as 5 feet 3 inches when fully grown (Brown et al., 1985). That might not seem tall by today's standards, but when we consider the height of previous hominins, it is very tall.

H. erectus also had a more advanced tool technology than *H. habilis*. The technology is called the Acheulean hand axe and is also considered part of the Lower Paleolithic period. Acheulean tools are more finely shaped than Oldowan tools. As we mentioned previously, Oldowan tools are generally modified on only one side of the stone. Acheulean tools usually have all edges modified as can be seen in Figure 2-7. Also, they show greater variety than Oldowan tools. Some have the "classic" teardrop-shaped form shown in the top of Figure 2.7; others are oval or narrower at the tip. The term "hand axe" implies that they were held in the hand for use, rather than being hafted to a wood or antler handle. They may have been used for a variety of purposes, such as cutting meat from the bone, disarticulating parts of animals for easier consumption, and breaking open bones for marrow. It is unlikely they were used for weapons, because they were usually too large to be hafted to a spear shaft and thrown. However, the animal bones found at *H. erectus* sites are often from the meatier parts of the animals, so they were probably involved in more active hunting.

Figure 2-6. *Homo erectus* specimen known as "Turkana Boy" (Image by Claire Houck).

Another accomplishment of *H. erectus* was the controlled use of fire. *H. erectus* was the first of our ancestors to have features recognizable as fire pits and they were typically located near Acheulean hand axes and butchered animal bones. Fire probably brought about huge changes to the quality of life for *H. erectus*. First, it would have allowed them to cook their meat, making it easier to chew and killing harmful bacteria. Second, it would have provided a source of light at night that would also have scared off predators. Finally, it provided heat, which is what enabled them to move north from Africa into colder climates. Thus, while *H. habilis* is the first of our ancestors to use stone tools, *H. erectus* is truly the first to use culture to adapt to their environment.

As we have discussed, *H. habilis* and *H. erectus* have the largest brain size of any of the previous hominins and in some cases the size overlapped with the low end of modern humans. It may be that their social structure was more complex, which may have been related to other developments, such as modern speech. In Chapter 1, we mentioned that some chimpanzees have been able to learn sign language to communicate. They certainly communicate vocally in the wild, but the studies done to try to teach chimpanzees spoken language were unsuccessful, largely because the physiology of their lips and vocal chords are not conducive to making human sounds. So, how can we tell when our earliest ancestors communicated in a more complex way? Research investigating the size of Broca's area (the part of the brain in the frontal lobe involved in speech) show that *H. habilis* had a larger area than Australopithecines and may have had the potential for more complex verbal communication. The even-larger brain of *H. erectus* suggests further development in language, but the shape of the hyoid bone (a U-shaped bone located below the floor of the mouth and the tongue and above the larynx) was more primitive than modern humans and so they probably did not have the full capability for modern speech (Capasso et al, 2008). It is not really until the Neanderthals (discussed in the next chapter), with their large brains and modern hyoids, that most scholars agree modern human speech (with its full range of vowels and consonants) was achieved (Lieberman, 2007).

Figure 2-7. Acheulean Tools from Kent, U.K.

2.4 BRINGING IT TOGETHER

In this chapter, we discussed the split between the non-human primates and our human ancestors, which scientists believe occurred over six million years ago in Africa. The key trait that initially separated us from non-human primates is that our ancestors began to walk on two legs instead of four. Following this change, our ancestors began to develop other characteristics, such as small lower faces, smaller canines, and (very gradually) larger brain sizes. The basal hominins are the first group to exhibit these characteristics, and they include the species identified as *Sahelanthropus tchadensis, Orroin tugenensis,* and *Ardipithecus ramidus*. Species evolving from these earliest ancestors were known as the Australopithecines and we discussed four species assigned to the genus *Australopithecus*, including *A. afarensis, A. anamensis, A. africanus,* and *A. garhi*. We also learned about the genus *Paranthropus* and how they probably represent an extinct branch of hominins. Next we explored the first species to be given the designation *Homo, Homo habilis*. *Homo habilis* has a much larger brain size than the previous hominins and, like *A. garhi*, uses stone tools known as Oldowan pebble choppers. Finally, we discussed *Homo erectus*, a specimen that has a much larger brain size than its predecessors and a more complicated tool technology (Acheulean), and is the first to develop controlled use of fire and is the first hominin to be found outside of Africa. We will continue to explore hominins and the eventual evolution of modern humans in the next chapter.

Key Terms and Concepts

Natural Selection — The concept developed by Charles Darwin to explain the mechanism for evolutionary changes.

Hominini — Used to describe modern humans and their ancestors. Also called hominins.

Basal hominins — Earliest of our human ancestors, appearing approximately 6 million years ago in Africa.

Sahelanthropus tchadensis — Earliest basal hominin from Chad, Africa.

Orrorin tugenensis — Basal hominin found in Kenya, Africa.

Ardipithecus ramidus — Basal hominin discovered in Ethiopia, Africa.

Australopithecines — Group of early hominins belonging to the genus *Australopithecus*.

Australopithecus afaransis — Australopithecine dating to 3.2 million years ago from Ethiopia, Africa.

Australopithecus anamensis — Australopithecine found in Kenya and dating between 4.2 and 3.9 million years ago.

Australopithecus africanus — Australopithecine from South Africa dating between 3 and 2 million years ago.

Australopithecus garhi — Australopithecine found in Ethiopia and dating to 2.5 million years ago. The first to use stone tools called Oldowan pebble choppers.

Oldowan pebble choppers — The first stone tools, used by *A. garhi* and *H. habilis*.

Lower Paleolithic period — Also known as the Early Stone Age, associated with the first use of stone tools.

Homo habilis — The first of our ancestors with the genus *Homo*, larger brain size than previous hominins and using Oldowan pebble choppers.

Homo erectus — A large-brained, more modern-looking hominin and the first to use Acheulean hand axes, control the use of fire, and leave Africa.

Broca's area — A part of the brain, like Wernicke's area, that has to do with speech.

Hyoid bone — A U-shaped bone located below the floor of the mouth and the tongue and above the larynx.

3: EARLY HUMANS

3.1 NEANDERTHALS

When we left off in Chapter 2, we had just finished talking about *Homo erectus* and the fact that they were the first of our ancestors to be found outside of Africa. As we discussed, this is largely due to their ability to control fire for cooking, light, and heat. The heat would have been particularly important, because as they moved north into Europe, the Middle East, and Asia, the climate would be much colder. This coldness was caused by the beginning of the Pleistocene epoch, also known as the last Ice Age. While the earth has been

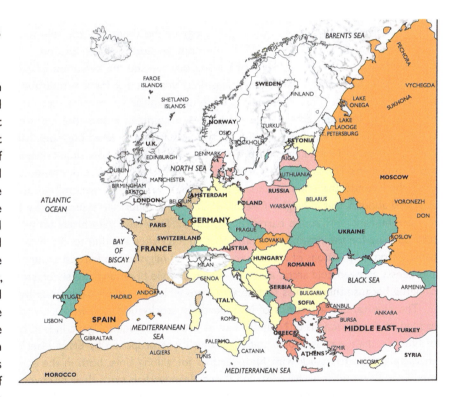

Figure 3-1. A map of Eurasia showing the location of the ice sheets during the Pleistocene epoch.

subjected to multiple ice ages over its history, the last one occurred between 2,588,000 and 11,700 years ago. Ice ages are characterized by a decrease in mean global temperature, the buildup of ice at the north and south poles, and a decrease in the levels of the oceans (due to much of the water becoming incorporated into the polar ice sheets).

Figure 3-2. Skull of *Homo neanderthalensis* (30,000–50,000 years old) (Image by Anagoria).

These changes meant that the world was a very different place from what we know today. In particular, the lowered sea levels meant that more of the continents were exposed, particularly the coastal areas and in some cases, island chains, such as those in Indonesia, were connected. The consequences for *H. erectus* traveling outside of Africa are that some areas of the world would have been more accessible. For example, walking from Africa to the Middle East and from Asia to Indonesia would have been possible because the lower sea levels meant everything was connected in a larger land mass. However, some areas would have been less accessible, such as northern Europe and Asia, due to the extension of the ice sheets. Many of us have the impression that the Ice Age was uniformly cold, but due to periods known as inter-glacials, the environment would be warmer, the ice sheets would melt slightly, and sea levels would rise. By understanding the climate and geology of the times, we are able to better understand where early hominin sites might be located.

It is during the Ice Age in parts of Europe that we see the evolution of our next hominin, *Homo neanderthalensis*, also known as Neanderthals. The first Neanderthal fossil recognized as such was discovered in the Neander valley of in 1856. Neanderthals are most similar to modern humans, compared to earlier hominins, because they have extremely large brain sizes, a complex stone tool culture, and they have adapted to an extremely harsh environment using cultural innovations. However, Neanderthals have clearly different physical features from modern humans (Figure 3-2). The first is a long, low skull compared to the high, narrow skull of modern humans. The average brain size for Neanderthals is about the same as modern humans and in some cases the Neanderthal brains were larger. Male Neanderthals are generally about 5 feet 5 inches tall and females averaged about 5 feet in height (Relethford, 2009). Neanderthals typically have a much stockier body type than modern humans, with round barrel-shaped chests. They have very heavy brow ridges and large nasal apertures (the opening for the nose). These physical characteristics are due to the Neanderthals evolving in an Ice Age climate from populations of *Homo erectus* who had migrated to Europe around 800,000 years ago. Large noses and chests allowed cold arctic air to be warmed while breathing and short, stocky bodies stay warmer in cold climates, because there is less surface area from which to lose valuable body heat.

The physical characteristics of Neanderthals' stocky bodies, low skulls with heavy brows, and large noses has led to the depictions of Neanderthals as brutish and unintelligent. In fact, one of the earliest classifications of Neanderthals was as "*Homo stupidus*," which was proposed by Ernst Haeckel in 1866 (Howell, 1957). This characterization has stuck with Neanderthals for a long time, both in the scientific literature and in popular media. However, what we have learned about Neanderthals since their discovery in the 19th century contradicts the brutish image of the hominin. The intelligence of Neanderthals can be seen in their advanced technology, adaptations to their environment, and closeness of their family ties.

Technologically, Neanderthals developed a new method for making stone tools that was much more complicated than previous techniques. Known as the Levallois technique, the method removes flakes from a prepared core (Figure 3-3). In contrast, the Acheulean technique (used by *H. erectus*) takes a large flake and shapes that into the desired form. The Levallois technique is more complicated, because a lot of work goes into preparing the core. Once the core is prepared, new tools can be easily removed from the core and are immediately ready for use. Stone tools made with the Levallois technique are part of the Mousterian industry, which is the stone tool industry associated with Neanderthals of the Middle Paleolithic period (or Middle Stone Age period). Neanderthals, unlike *Homo erectus*, had a much greater variety of tools used for different purposes. Special tools were made for spear points, carving wood and bone, scraping hides, and butchering animals.

Neanderthal hunting methods can be inferred from the type of stone tools and animal remains found at sites in Europe and the Middle East. Spear points were typically large and probably hafted to heavy spears. The spears were most likely used as thrusting spears, rather than throwing spears. This means that Neanderthals would have had to get close to their prey—something that was probably often dangerous. Neanderthals may also have driven prey over cliffs, as is evident at the site of La Cotte de St. Brelade. At this site, excavators uncovered the remains of 20 mammoths and five woolly rhinos at the base of a cliff (Chazan, 2011; Scott, 1986). The animals could have been startled by shouting or by waving torches, stampeded over the cliff, and then butchered once dead at the base of the cliff with much less danger to the Neanderthals. Not surprisingly, given the Ice Age conditions, the Neanderthal diet was probably mostly meat, with some studies suggesting that the amount of meat in the diet was as high as 97% (Balter et al., 2002; Richards et al., 2000).

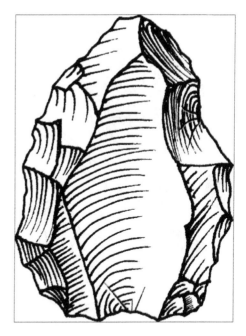

Figure 3-3. Levallois Core.

Adaptations to the environment include clothing and the use of caves for shelter. These items would have been particularly important in the Ice Age climate, with its long, cold winters and short, cool summers. Unfortunately, clothing does not preserve well, so our conclusions about what kinds of clothing they had are based on the stone and bone tools from their sites. Studies on what Neanderthals wore conclude that they would have needed tailored clothing and that "...an animal skin across the shoulder would not have sufficed" (Sorensen, 2009:2201). Clothing and foot coverings would have to keep out cold air and snow in order to be effective. Awls (bone tools with a sharpened end) are found at Neanderthal sites and could have been used to put holes in hides, and then thin strips of hide could have been used to assemble the clothing and shoes. As mentioned previously, Neanderthal sites have remains from animals such as caribou, bison, and mammoth, whose hides would provide warm clothing, shoes, sleeping mats, and blankets.

Excavations of Neanderthal cave sites show that there were different activity areas within the sites and they were not haphazardly used or arranged. Generally, depending on the natural structure of the cave, firepits and cooking areas are located in the center and toward the front of the cave. This would allow smoke to be vented out the front of the cave, but the fire would still be centralized enough for heat and light. Often, Neanderthal caves were used repeatedly over many millennia, and Neanderthals would occupy a cave from a period of several days to several weeks and then move on. Later—sometimes years, sometimes decades would pass—they would reoccupy the site, setting it up in much the same way as they had previously. At sites, such as Grotte XVI (Cave Sixteen) in France, the fires areas (also called combustion zones) were in the front center of the cave, sleeping areas were probably near the fires, butchering and stone tool–making activities took place near the mouth of the cave, and refuse could be discarded out the front, along the sides, or toward the back of the cave (Rigaud et al., 1995).

Another question you might have about Neanderthals is: what were their families like? The closeness of their families can be seen in the care given to their sick and elderly, several of whom survived tragic injury and illness to live well beyond their life expectancy. One specimen that shows a high degree of care after injury is Shanidar 1.

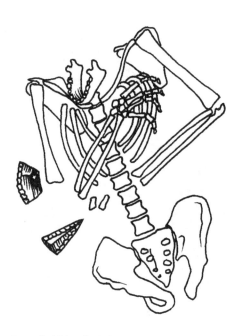

Figure 3-4. Neanderthal burial at Kebara Cave, Israel

Shanidar 1, from Shanidar Cave in Iraq, was an adult male between 40 and 50 years old (which is very old for a Neanderthal). He had received a blow to the left side of his head that crushed his left eye orbit and probably left him blind in that eye. His right arm was also amputated below the elbow. Finally, damage in his lower left leg and foot suggest he walked with a permanent limp (Stewart, 1977). Yet, he survived and lived to a ripe old age. Why did they keep him alive? He certainly was not able to hunt, nor would have been much use with daily chores, such as getting water and firewood and preparing food. He may have played a role as a story teller or a shaman (a spiritual leader). This is also not the only case of a Neanderthal surviving to old age with severe injuries or illness. The site of La Chapelle-aux-Saints Cave in France contained a Neanderthal skeleton called the "Old Man of La Chapelle" from an adult male between 25 and 40 years old. Initial examination of the skeleton after it was discovered in the early 1900s led to the depiction of a bowlegged, bent-backed Neanderthal with a brutish demeanor. Later research showed that the Neanderthal specimen from La Chapelle suffered severe arthritis and tooth loss (Trinkaus, 1985). Negotiating the Ice Age environment with such severe arthritis would have been difficult, as would chewing meat with only a few teeth, so he likely had help moving about and breaking down his food into bites that could be easily chewed.

Neanderthals were also the first hominins to bury their dead. At several sites, such as Kebara and Amud caves in modern-day Israel, individuals were buried with grave goods such as stone tools and animal bones (Figure 3-4). At a cave called Shanidar in Iraq, the skeleton of an adult male aged from 30–45 years was discovered lying on his left side in a fetal position. A study of soil samples from the burial indicated that flowers were placed in the grave (Solecki, 1975). The care given to the deceased shows that they were cared for in life and that Neanderthals may have believed in an afterlife. The Neanderthal burials are certainly the earliest evidence we have for ritualized behavior in hominins.

We discussed how Neanderthals made clothing and shoes to survive in the Ice Age, but did they ever make objects that were used for decorative purposes? Not really. No examples of a bone or stone carved into a particular shape other than used for hunting or for another purpose have been found to date, nor are there any examples of abstract carvings. However, new data on the age of cave paintings (discussed later in this chapter) in Spain suggest that cave art could have first been made by Neanderthals. Three images were dated to between 40,000 and 35,000 years ago, which is 10,000–15,000 years earlier than previously thought. The images are a red disc, a hand stencil, and a club-shaped symbol (Pike et al., 2012). Anatomically modern humans were also found in this region of Spain 40,000 years ago, so it is unclear yet whether or not Neanderthals were truly responsible for the paintings. However, given the other modern traits shown by Neanderthals, such as advanced technologies, burial of the dead, and care for the sick and injured, it may be that they also had begun to create art.

Now that we have gained some understanding about what Neanderthals looked like and learned about some of their behaviors, the next question is: Were Neanderthals ancestral to modern humans? There are three scenarios proposed for the origin of Neanderthals and their relationship to modern humans. The first is that Neanderthals evolved from *Homo erectus* populations in Europe independently from modern humans. In this scenario, the last common ancestor shared with modern humans is *Homo erectus* between 300,000 and 700,000 years ago. The second scenario suggests that there was an intermediate species evolved from *Homo erectus* known as *Homo antecessor*. *Homo antecessor* then evolved into *Homo neanderthalensis*. However, there are only fragmentary remains of *Homo antecessor* from Spain and more data are needed to support the claim of an intermediate species. Finally, the last scenario argues that Neanderthals and modern humans did evolve separately (Neanderthals in Europe and modern humans in Africa), but when modern humans migrated to Europe, the two groups were similar enough to mate and produce offspring. One specimen in particular, the "Lagar Velho boy," is a skeleton of a 4-year-old boy with both Neanderthal (short, stocky legs) and modern human (a chin and a high domed skull) traits (Zilhão and Trinkaus, 2002).

While archaeological data such as stone tools, skeletal remains, and sites have been useful in identifying the life ways of Neanderthals, one other avenue of exploration helps us understand the evolutionary relationship of some hominins. This is genetic data. Genetic data can be extracted from Neanderthal and early modern human bone that has not completely fossilized. Specifically, mitochondrial DNA (DNA inherited through the maternal line) studies have suggested that Neanderthals evolved independently of modern humans (Greene et al., 2010), but that there are some Neanderthal traits that were passed on through interbreeding. In fact, the study by Greene et al. suggested that 1%–4% of most people of Eurasian descent carry some Neanderthal in them.

So, what happened to the Neanderthals? We know they lived in Europe and the Middle East between 400,000 and 30,000 years ago. They had evolved a lifestyle that was uniquely adapted to the Ice Age environment, but after about 30,000 years ago, we see no evidence of Neanderthals on the landscape and the only hominin species left is *Homo sapiens* (modern humans). Neanderthals lived in small populations and probably had a slow reproductive rate. Once modern humans moved into regions they occupied, they would have to compete for food and other resources with these new hominins. It may be that they were not able to adapt to such a change in circumstances quickly enough. Researchers have suggested that the last known Neanderthal site, Gorham's Cave in Gibraltar, is indicative of a species literally pushed to the edge of its territory. Another possibility is that Neanderthals did not go extinct per se, but interbred with modern humans and their smaller population was eventually absorbed into the larger, modern human population. Neanderthals will continue to be a mystery to archaeologists for many years to come.

3.2 EARLY MODERN HUMANS

As mentioned in this chapter, early modern humans (also known as anatomically modern humans) evolved independently of Neanderthals. But how did this come about? There are three hypotheses that compete to explain the origins of modern humans. The first, and currently least supported, is the "Multi-Regional model". This model contends that early modern humans evolved from archaic humans in different regions and gene flow between groups kept the evolution continuous through archaic to modern forms. Supporters of this model argue that there are morphological traits that change gradually over time, suggesting a slow, gradual evolution from *Homo erectus* to Neanderthals to early modern humans to modern humans (Wolpoff et al., 2001). The second is known as the "Out of Africa model". This states that between 200,000 and 150,000 years ago, archaic *Homo sapiens* evolved to anatomically modern humans solely in Africa. Fossil evidence of early modern humans from Africa predates specimens found in other parts of the world. Also, genetic evidence (mtDNA and Y-chromosomal DNA) supports that modern humans evolved from *Homo erectus* over 160,000 years ago in Africa. A final model is known as the "Mostly Out of Africa," or "Hybridization," model. In this model, the idea that modern humans first arose in Africa and then spread out is accepted, but supporters argue that modern humans interbred with archaic species such as Neanderthals. The evidence for this model comes from the previously mentioned fossil data with

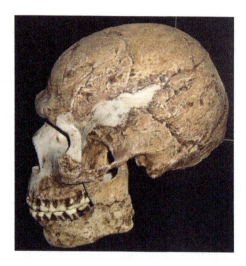

Figure 3-5. Skuhl V skull from Qafzeh Cave, Israel (Image by Wapondaponda).

Figure 3-6. Male Cro-Magnon skull from Bichon Cave, Switzerland (Image by Latenium).

modern and Neanderthal traits and the genetic data showing modern humans with some Neanderthal genes (Relethford, 2009). More data continue to be uncovered and the models will probably be modified as evidence comes to light, but currently, it seems the "Mostly Out of Africa" model is the best supported by fossil evidence and genetic data.

Early modern humans are virtually indistinguishable from modern humans living today. Their high domed skulls, vertical foreheads, reduced brow ridges, and pronounced chins signified their differences from archaic forms such as Neanderthals and *Homo erectus*. The post-cranium (lower body) of modern humans is also different. In general, modern humans are taller, less stocky, and less muscular than the archaic. Some early modern human skeletons exhibit a mix of archaic and modern traits, such as Skuhl V from Qafzeh cave in Israel, which dates to around 90,000 years ago (Figure 3-5). Other early modern human skeletons show more recent traits, such as the 13,000-year-old "Cro-Magnon" skull from Bichon Cave, Switzerland (Figure 3-6). The term "Cro-Magnon" is often used as a synonym for early modern humans, because the first early modern human skulls were identified from the site of Cro-Magnon in France.

3.3 THE UPPER PALEOLITHIC

Early modern human life ways are particularly fascinating because we can gain insight into what differentiated modern humans from their predecessors. Early modern human culture is significant for advances in technology, burial rituals, and art. This fluorescence of creativity is known as the Upper Paleolithic period. Some of the distinguishing features of the technology of this era are the use of microlithic stone tools and an increase in the use of bone tools. Microlithic stone tools (or microliths) are small blades that are inserted into bone, wood, or antler shafts to make composite tools such as projectiles (spears), scrapers, and knives. The bone and antler tools are finely crafted harpoons, needles, awls, and fish hooks. Also, decorative bone and antler objects were made and either worn as pendants or sewn onto clothing. A major innovation was the invention of the atlatl, or spear

Figure 3-7. An atlatl (spear thrower).

thrower. These bone or wood shafts with a hook on the end were used to throw light spears. The dynamics of the atlatl are such that it increases the distance and force with which a spear can be thrown (Figure 3-7).

Burial rituals also become much more elaborate in the Upper Paleolithic period. I mentioned previously that Neanderthals buried their dead sometimes and on occasion they would include burial goods within the grave, but modern human burial rituals were much more involved. For example, an Upper Paleolithic habitation and burial site in Predmostí (Czech Republic) contained 20 burials (Svoboda, 2008). These burials included stone tools and animal bones, including mammoth, reindeer, wolf, bear, fox, hare, and wolverine. Decorative objects were also found, including bone beads and perforated carnivore teeth. Another burial, from Goat's Hole Cave, Wales, contained an adult male around 21 years old buried with a mammoth's skull, ivory rods, and shells. At some of these sites, there appear to be differences in the number of burial goods associated with different individuals, which may indicate that some individuals had higher status in their society.

One of the most exciting aspects of the Upper Paleolithic period is the fluorescence of art beginning around 40,000 years ago. There are two main kinds of art during this period. The first is mobile art, which is art that can be moved from place to place. As mentioned above in regards to burials, bone beads and perforated teeth were found interred with some individuals. Also, carvings of animals on bone or stone are found at some sites. Animals represented include mammoths, bison, and horses and often these images are very naturalistic and suggest movement in the lines and positioning of the animals. One piece from the Mas-d'Azil site in France is a short baton or staff with three horse heads on it. One is of a small or "young" horse, one is of a large or "adult" horse, and the final horse head appears to be decaying or defleshed. The interpretation is that it shows the stages of life—from birth, to adulthood, to death.

A more thought-provoking type of mobile art is the Venus figurines. These are female shapes, carved out of stone or bone, which exaggerate the secondary sexual characteristics (such as breasts, abdomen, and hips) and de-emphasize the other features of the female form (such as head, legs, and arms). One of the most famous of these is the "Venus of Willendorf," which is a 10-cm-high statue of a woman with no facial features, a hint of hands above the breasts, and legs that end with no feet (Figure 3-8). The Figure dates to around 24,000 years ago and was found in the early 1900s in Austria. The exaggeration of the breasts, hips, and abdomen on this specimen has led scholars to surmise that it was a fertility figure. Other interpretations are that the people of the Upper Paleolithic idealized women. Yet another theory is that they represent goddesses or religious figures. I have also had students who suggested that they were Upper Paleolithic Barbies and represent an idealized female form. Other Venus figurines include the Venus of Dolní Věstonice (Czech

Figure 3-8. Venus of Willendorf (Image by Mathias Kabel).

Republic), the Venus of Brassempouy (from France, with infrequently depicted facial features), and the Venus of Laussel (also from France, carved in bas-relief and holding a bison or auroch horn).

The other form of art in the Upper Paleolithic art is parietal art. This art is found on the walls and ceilings of caves in France and Spain and on cliff faces in Australia and Africa. These paintings generally represent animals, with some geometric and, very rarely, humanoid shapes (Scarre, 2005). The cave paintings of France and Spain are done exclusively in sites that do not contain habitation debris. Also, many of the caves have certain themes or animals represented. Finally, most of the caves were visited repeatedly to add more paintings. One of the oldest cave art sites is Chauvet Cave in the southeastern part of France. Discovered in 1994, the cave contains hundreds of paintings made out of minerals (red and yellow ochre) and charcoal ground up and mixed with water. The paintings were made with animal hair brushes, by dipping fingers into the paint, and by blowing the paint onto the wall, possibly through a bird bone tube. Unlike other cave art sites, which typically depict herbivores such as bison, horses, and reindeer, Chauvet cave has many representations of carnivores such as cave bears, hyenas, lions, and panthers. Another famous cave site that depicts mostly bison is Altamira Cave in Spain. The cave was found in 1879 and was the first site to attribute art to Upper Paleolithic humans. Finally, Lascaux Cave is probably one of the most famous sites. Located in the southwest of France in the Dordogne River valley, the cave was discovered by four young men in 1940. Studied extensively, then opened to the public, the cave was closed in 1963 due to the damage to the paintings from high levels of carbon dioxide from visitors. A replica of the two main halls was constructed in the early 1980s for visitors and the "real" Lascaux was available only to researchers. The paintings of Lascaux date to around 17,300 years ago and number around 2,000. The images that are depicted include aurochs (extinct cattle), Pleistocene horses, elk, bison, as well as some abstract designs (Figure 3-9). A rare human and bird figure is depicted in a portion of the cave called the "shaft." This image is rare because it may represent an actual event of a man being killed by an injured bison. If you look closely at the stomach of the bison, it appears to have entrails coming out of the stomach, possibly caused by a spear throw to the stomach. The human appears to have fallen or is falling and black lines suggest dropped spears. The bird totem is depicted below the human figure and both the bird and the human have the same shaped head. The bird figure, in particular, is difficult to interpret, but in some more recent cultures, bird imagery represents the transition from life to death (Figure 3-10).

Why did humans go through so much trouble to create this art and who in their society created it? There are several theories as to why humans created this art. The first is, of course, "art for art's sake," which basically means that early modern humans had an artistic urge to create things. The paintings certainly show a high degree of skill, with the animals moving and depicted very life-like. Another theory is that there were created during religious trances by shamans or spiritual leaders. Related to this, the drawings may have been a form of "sympathetic magic," where a person can influence something based on its relationship or resemblance to another thing, such as invoking a successful hunt by drawing the animal you want to kill and a line representing a spear going into that animal. Also, some of the horses have large bellies. This may be how they looked, or it could be pregnant animals representing plentiful prey. Finally, it may have been for the education of children. Chauvet Cave in southwestern France is a cave that has paintings over 30,000 years old and also has footprints preserved in solidified cave sediment that represents an 8- to 10-year-old child. The Pleistocene was a dangerous time and hunting a dangerous lifestyle, so it may have

Figure 3-9. Image of extinct Elk stag (Megaloceros) with abstract design.

been a means to show children how to hunt certain prey. This last hypothesis relates to who made the cave art. Because most of the images represent prey species, it has long been assumed that men were drawing the images. However, hand stencils (made by placing a hand on the wall and blowing paint through a tube) come in all sizes. While it is impossible to tell sex based on a handprint, the variable sizes suggest multiple members of the society were entering the caves. We will probably never know the exact reason behind the painting of caves in the Upper Paleolithic, but it gives us much food for thought to speculate on the behavior of early modern humans.

Figure 3-10. Human and Bird Figure in shaft panel (Image by Peter80).

3.4 BRINGING IT TOGETHER

In this chapter we explored the origins and development of the Neanderthals, including their specific adaptations to Ice Age conditions, their advanced technology compared to other hominins, and their evolutionary relationship to modern humans. Neanderthals have fascinated us since their discovery in the 1800s and there has been a lot of speculation on what they were like—from brutish beasts to hominins very similar to us. We also learned that the Neanderthals disappeared around 30,000 years ago, soon after the arrival of modern humans in Europe. There is speculation on whether or not modern humans and Neanderthals interbred, but most scholars accept that modern humans evolved in Africa around 200,000 years ago and spread to other areas of the world. These early modern humans exhibited new levels of sophistication in technology, burial rituals, and art. The Venus figurines represent goddess or fertility figures that may indicate early religion. The parietal art on cave walls show a refined knowledge of the animals in their environment and a need for expression in an artistic form, as well as some practical purposes such as educating their children about the world around them. The evolution and disappearance of Neanderthals and the emergence of modern humans as the only hominin species on earth represents an amazing chapter in the history of humanity.

Key Terms and Concepts

Pleistocene epoch	The last Ice Age, occurred between 2,588,000 and 11,700 years ago.
Neandethals	*Homo neanderthalensis*, an archaic form of human evolving in Europe around 400,000 years ago and disappearing around 30,000 years ago.
Levallois technique	The method removes flakes from a prepared core, used by Neanderthals.
Mousterian industry	Includes the Levallois technique and is the stone tool industry associated with Neanderthals of the Middle Paleolithic period.

Middle Paleolithic period	Middle Stone Age period associated with Neanderthals.
Shanidar 1	A Neanderthal male from Shanidar Cave, aged between 40 and 50 years, blind in one eye and with one arm, his skeleton suggests that Neanderthals cared for their injured.
"Old Man of La Chapelle"	Adult male Neanderthal between 25 and 40 years old, who suffered from severe arthritis and tooth loss, also indicates Neanderthals cared for their injured.
Neanderthal burials	Neanderthals were the first hominin to bury their dead, seen at sites like Shanidar and Kebara.
"Lagar Velho boy"	Is a skeleton of a 4-year-old boy with both Neanderthal and modern human traits dating to 24,000 years ago. May be an example of hybridization.
"Multi-regional" model	Early modern humans evolved in different regions and gene flow between groups kept the evolution continuous through early to late forms.
"Out of Africa" model	The second model of modern human origins, which states that between 200,000 and 150,000 years ago, archaic *Homo sapiens* evolved to anatomically modern humans solely in Africa.
"Mostly Out of Africa" model	Also known as the Hybridization model, modern humans first arose in Africa and then spread out, but modern humans interbred with archaic species such as Neanderthals.
Cro-Magnon	Often used as a synonym for early modern humans, because the first early modern human skulls were identified from the site of Cro-Magnon in France.
Microlithic stone tools	Also known as microliths. These are small blades that are inserted into bone, wood, or antler shafts to make composite tools.
Atlatl	Or spear thrower, a bone or wood shaft with a hook on the end used to throw spears.
Mobile Art	Art work that can be moved from place to place.
"Venus figurines"	These are female shapes, carved out of stone or bone, which exaggerate the secondary sexual characteristics.
Parietal Art	Art work on cave walls or cliff faces. Famous cave art sites include Chauvet Cave, Altamira Cave, and Lascaux Cave.
"Sympathetic Magic"	One can influence something based on its relationship to another thing, such as invoking a successful hunt by drawing the animal you want to kill.

4: HUMAN EXPANSION

4.1 HUMAN MIGRATION TO AUSTRALIA

Now that we have completed the story of early human evolution, it is time to follow the migration of early modern humans to occupy the rest of the world. As we discussed in Chapter 3, the initial migration of hominins out of Africa was made easier by the lowered sea levels of the Ice Age. We discussed how *Homo erectus* left Africa around one million years ago and spread out to Europe, the Middle East, and Asia. Then, early modern humans (*Homo sapiens*) evolved in Africa and spread out to those same areas, replacing and possibly mating with archaic humans (such as Neanderthals). Early modern humans continue to spread to areas previously unoccupied by hominins, such as Australia and the Americas. In the travel to the Americas, due to the lower sea levels, there was a land bridge connecting what is now Siberia to modern-day Alaska. However, travel to Australia was a different matter.

What made the journey to Australia different is that at no time during the last Ice Age was Australia connected to Southeast Asia. The landmass connecting the Indonesian Islands to Southeast Asia is known as Sunda and the landmass connecting Australia, New Guinea, and Tasmania is known as Sahul (Figure 4-1). A 55-mile-wide channel separated Southeast Asia from Australia and, therefore, early modern humans would have needed water transport to get from one place to another. There were a series of islands between these two landmasses, known as Wallacea (named after Alfred Russel Wallace, a British naturalist), but the distance would still have been too great to swim across. Although no boats have been found, this is not surprising, given that they were probably made of wood and would not preserve. So, we have to assume that people made boats out of wood and other materials that would have decayed over time.

There were two possible routes for modern humans crossing Wallacea into Sahul and it is difficult to know which routes were used. It is mostly likely that the people used the small islands in Wallacea to "hop" across from Sunda to Sahul. This meant that there would generally be no more than about six miles between islands. The advantages of "island hopping" are that there was less water to traverse and the islands would have provided resources, such as food and fresh water. The second route would have been more to the south and gone directly across from Sunda to Sahul. This more direct route would have required crossing around 62 miles of open sea. It is unclear why people ventured from one territory across open water into a new land, but perhaps the population

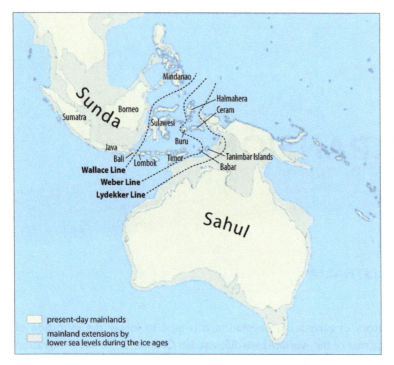

Figure 4-1. Map of the Sahul and Sunda landmasses (Image by Maximilian Dörrbecker).

was getting high in Sunda and people needed to move on to have more territory for hunting. Also, people could have gradually ventured out further and further with fishing boats until they found new land teeming with game. Regardless of the route taken or reasons for migrating, there is evidence of habitation on coastal Australia at around 50,000 years ago and there was a large enough initial population to expand across the continent.

Currently, the oldest site in Australia is Nauwalabila I, dating to around 50,000 years ago, which is a rock shelter located in the northwestern section of Australia (Chazan, 2011). The site contained charcoal from firepits and flakes from making stone tools. Another ancient Australian site is Lake Mungo, which dates to between 40,000 and 50,000 years ago. The remains of the earliest known cremated human (an adult female) were found at the Lake Mungo site in the late 1960s. Another early site is called Devil's Lair, located in Western Australia, which dates to between 41,000 and 46,000 years ago. Devil's Lair is a cave that contained hearths, but few stone tools or animal remains. Another early site in what is now New Guinea is known as Bobongara Hill. The site dates to about 40,000 years ago; researchers found hundreds of axes in and around the site. Researchers speculated that these stone axes were used for clearing trees (Groube et al., 1989). The open spaces would have allowed small villages to be erected and the logs from the trees would be useful for boats or wooden structures.

Later Australian sites show increasing complexity in the burial patterns and material culture. For example, at the Roonka site, located in southeastern Australia, the lower levels date to around 16,000 to 20,000 years ago. The burials of at least three individuals were found in the lower levels of the site (Robertson and Prescott, 2006). According to archaeological findings, the site was abandoned after this initial occupation and reoccupied around 10,000 years ago. Skeletal remains dating after 10,000 years ago come from more than 200 individuals. Some of the burials show greater care than others and were buried with elaborate artifacts, such as a kangaroo-tooth headband. Another site with complex burials is Coobool Creek, which is located near the Roonka site and contained 126 individuals. What was interesting about Coobool Creek is that some of the burials had evidence of cranial deformation (Durband, 2008). Cranial deformation is the permanent alteration

Figure 4-2. Skull from Peru showing cranial deformation (Image by Didier Descouens).

of the skull by binding with cloth and is done to individuals from infancy and continued until the individual reaches maturity. It results in a conical-shaped cranium as shown in an example from Peru in Figure 4-2. Cranial deformation is typically done to indicate group affiliation or social status and does not affect the development of the brain. It does take quite a lot of work on the parents' part and the fact that not all the skulls from Coobool Creek have cranial deformation indicates that it may have been used to signify individuals of higher status in the group.

Ancient Australians never developed agriculture, but continued to develop an increasingly complex culture with changing stone-tool technology. Also, while they did not record their histories in writing, they did leave a rich record of rock art on cave walls and cliff faces (Figure 4-3). Some of the most

Figure 4-3. Rock art from Namadgi National Park, Australia (Image by Martyman at English Language Wikipedia).

well-studied paintings, known as the Bradshaw paintings (after their European discoverer) or Gwion Gwion (by Australian Aborigines), are found in caves in Western Australia. Dating over 16,000 years ago, the paintings depict human figures with headdresses. Another site in Western Australia, called Gunbilngmurrung, has a beeswax turtle on a rock-shelter wall dating to about 4,000 years ago. The practice of creating rock art is clearly of great antiquity and continued well past the arrival of Europeans in Australia.

4.2 THE FIRST AMERICANS

Another place to be colonized during the Late Pleistocene is the Americas. The peopling of the New World has been a question of great interest ever since Europeans arrived in the Americas. Where did these people come from? How did they get here? Scientists have been puzzling over this for centuries and there is still debate on some of the issues. There are three main theories regarding the timing for the arrival of humans in the Americas. The first to be proposed was the Clovis first model (or short chronology) and this model contends that humans arrived no later than 13,500 years ago. Another model is the Pre-Clovis model (or long chronology) and this suggests that humans arrived over 20,000 years ago. Finally, the Early Arrival model argues that humans were in the Americas as early as 40,000 years ago. Other theories are also used to debate the route that was taken into the Americas. These are the Bering Land Bridge, the Pacific Coastal Migration route, and the Atlantic Migration.

The earliest theory on the time when the first people arrived in the Americas is known as the Clovis first model. This theory is named after a town in New Mexico, where, at nearby site, extinct animal bones were found associated with stone tools. The site also yielded distinct spear points, known as Clovis points, which were long and straight-sided with a flute or flake taken from the base (Figure 4-5). Since their discovery at the site in the 1930s, these points have been recovered throughout North, Middle and South America. Sites with Clovis points range in age from 13,500 to 12,500 years ago and often contain extinct animals bones, such as mammoth, mastodon, *Bison antiquus* (an extinct species of bison), and Pleistocene horse. The Clovis sites are often also

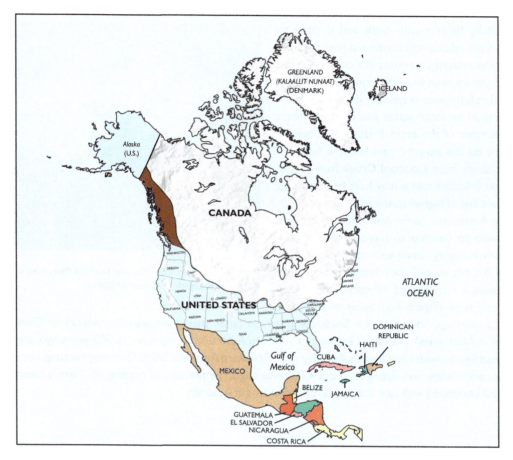

Figure 4-4. Map of North America showing the extent of the Ice sheets during the Pleistocene epoch.

referred to as belonging to a Clovis culture. This is not to imply that one group moved over such a huge territory, but that many groups with the same technology hunted and gathered in the Americas.

The Clovis first theory was supported in the archaeological community for over 40 years, however, in the 1970s; several sites were discovered that did not fit the Clovis first model. The first site that did not fit this pattern was Meadowcroft Rockshelter, located in western Pennsylvania. Meadowcroft Rockshelter was excavated by students from the University of Pittsburgh and directed by James Adovasio. Findings from the excavations revealed that the rockshelter was occupied for over 19,000 years (Adovasio et al., 1990). Unfortunately, after the dates for the site were published, many archaeologists did not agree with the findings and argued that the radiocarbon dates were contaminated by water from nearby coal beds. Also, no Pleistocene fauna have been found in association with the earliest levels of the site. However, subsequent radiocarbon dates and testing found that there was very little chance of the deposits being contaminated and Meadowcroft Rockshelter is now considered a Pre-Clovis site.

Another site considered a Pre-Clovis site in the Americas is Cactus Hill in Virginia, which was discovered in the early 21st century. Cactus Hill is an extremely small site, probably an overnight camp site that contained stone tools and a hearth. The dates from charcoal in the hearth range from 15,000 to 17,000 years old. This older material was found beneath an occupation that contained the characteristic Clovis points of the Clovis culture. A site of similar age, called the Topper site, from South Carolina contained artifacts below the Clovis levels.

In Chile, South America, a site called Monte Verde was discovered in 1975 and excavated by a team led by Tom Dillehay. The site was remarkable for its excellent preservation (it is located in a bog, which is an anaerobic environment preventing decay of organics) and its antiquity: dating to around 15,000 years ago. Artifacts from the site included stakes from wood and hide structures, mastodon hides and meat, local and non-local plant remains, and salt from the coast. Dillehay's conclusion is that the site was occupied for a fairly long period of time (several months) by about 20–30 people (Dillehay, 1989). The structures had hearths on the inside that were lined with clay, as well as larger hearths outside the structures. The variety of plants (including species with medicinal uses) suggests that people had a keen understanding of the resources in their environment. Thus, not only did Monte Verde predate the oldest dates for Clovis, but the type and variety of artifacts indicate they had probably arrived in Chile a long time before occupying the Monte Verde site.

Figure 4-5. Example of a Clovis Point.

Some other sites, many of which are controversial, have been used to support the hypothesis that humans may have arrived in the Americas between 30,000 and 40,000 years ago. One of these sites is the Pedra Furada site in Brazil. Located in the Serra da Capivara National Park, the site is actually a series of rock shelters. Excavations at one rock shelter dated between 32,000 and 48,000 years ago. Burnt areas and worked cobbles are the only signs of human activity at the site and some archaeologists have suggested that the burnt areas are natural brush fires and the worked cobbles were not deliberately shaped by humans. Other early arrival sites are the Bluefish Caves in western Canada that contained worked mammoth bone dating to around 28,000 years ago. Critics of this site argue that the mammoth remains are isolated finds and are not in context with human activity. Finally, the previously mentioned site of Monte Verde has an area of the site with a hearth and some stone tools that were radiocarbon dated to over 30,000 years ago. While the excavators of Monte Verde feel that the excavation and dating methods are valid, the researchers at Monte Verde believe that further research is needed in this area of the site.

Currently, most scholars fall into the Pre-Clovis model for the arrival of humans in the Americas. However, as mentioned previously, there are various theories for the route that was taken into the Americas. The possible routes have a lot to do with variations in the Ice Age environment. As we discussed with the peopling of Australia, the Ice Age environment connected some land masses due to lower sea levels. In the case of the Americas, the current regions of Siberia and Alaska were connected by a land bridge known as Beringia or the Bering Land Bridge. This land bridge was actually hundreds of miles across and used by migratory birds and animals, as well as humans. However, during warmer times in the Late Pleistocene, the land bridge would have been submerged as the ice sheets melted. Geologists have provided archaeologists with information regarding these changes and Beringia would have been submerged briefly from 34,000 to 30,000 years ago and becoming submerged between 12,000 and 10,000 years ago. However, as we discussed with Australia, humans were on the move and populations had expanded so people needed to seek out new territories for hunting and gathering. The migratory animals, in particular, would have provided a strong incentive for moving into new territories. Thus, the Bering Land Bridge would have been a viable option for people coming into the Americas.

Figure 4-6. Example of a Solutrean point.

Another factor with the Land Bridge theory is that there were two ice sheets, known as the Cordilleran and the Laurentide, covering most of northern North America. The Cordilleran ice sheet covered the north Pacific Coast, including the Cascade Mountain range, and the Laurentide ice sheet covered the middle and eastern parts of Canada and the northern U.S. At times of glacial maximum, these two ice sheets met, which would preclude people from traveling into the rest of North America. The last glacial maximum occurred between 26,000 and 20,000 years ago. Thus, while it was possible that people could live in Beringia and a small portion of Canada and Alaska during this time, there was about a 6,000-year period when travel between the ice sheets (also known as the ice free corridor) would have been impossible.

Other routes may have been possible for entry into the Americas. In particular, a Pacific Coastal route would have been a viable option. As was discussed with Australia, people most probably had boats that could be used to travel short distances. Just as the first Australians island hopped across Wallacea, the first Americans may have used boats to travel up the coast of East Asia and down the coast of northwestern North America into more southerly, ice-free portions of the continent. The location of sites such as Monte Verde, Chile, Arlington Springs, Clear Lake, and Borax Lake (the latter three are in California) near coasts supports this hypothesis. However, it is difficult to tell if there may have been additional early sites, because the water levels have risen over 300 feet since the end of the Ice Age.

Another hypothesis about how people came to the Americas is the Atlantic Crossing (also known as the Solutrean Hypothesis). This hypothesis was proposed by Dennis Stanford and Bruce Bradley (2004). According to this hypothesis, people associated with a culture known as the Solutrean in Europe migrated to North America. The key link for thinking that these two cultures are associated is the same method for making stone tools. Both the Solutrean and Clovis points are made with a method known as the "over-shot technique," which results in a series of diagonal channels spanning the width of the blade (Figure 4-6). Stanford and Bradley argue that there are no known counterparts to this technique in Eastern Asia, Siberia, or Beringia (areas where early Americans are thought to have migrated from). Some archaeologists have criticized this hypothesis, arguing that the similarities are too slight to be a direct link. Also, the Atlantic crossing would have been much more hazardous, because, unlike the Pacific coast, pack ice obscured the northern part of the Atlantic Ocean all year long, so there would have been no relief from the ice or north Atlantic waters. However, Stanford and Bradley argue that Inuit people (sea-mammal hunters from northern Canada and Alaska) traditionally spent months out at sea hunting seals and small whales without ever returning to dry land, so we know it is possible to live and hunt on the pack ice. Also, the presence of many early sites in the eastern part of the U.S., such as Cactus Hill, and Meadowcroft, may suggest an Atlantic crossing.

Regardless of when and how people came to the Americas, another pressing question is what did the earliest Americans look like? For example, did they look like modern Native Americans or did they resemble a variety of different groups? There are only a handful of Native American skeletons that date between 9,000 and 10,000 years ago and none (so far) that predate 10,000 years ago. Of the 13 skeletons currently dated to as old as 9,000–10,000 years, one is the most controversial. This is the specimen known as Kennewick Man that was found in 1996 along the Columbia River in Washington State. Discovered by sightseers and brought to the attention of authorities, the Kennewick Man skeleton was eventually examined by a forensics expert (Chatters, 2002). The initial observation was that the skeleton was in excellent condition and might be fairly recent, but subsequent radiocarbon dating revealed that the skeleton dated to 9,300 years. Also, forensic examination revealed a three-inch projectile point embedded in the hip bone. A computed axial tomography (CAT) scan revealed that this was a spear point called a Cascade point and was made between 7,500 and 12,000 years ago. However, it was not the age of the skeleton that proved controversial, but the conclusions about ancestry. Initial analysis determined that the skeleton was a male of European or Middle Eastern ancestry (known as Caucasoid in forensic analysis). Further analysis revealed the skeleton more closely resembled ancient Japanese or Polynesians (specifically a tribe in Japan known as the Ainu). One of the groups that Kennewick Man did not resemble is that of modern Native Americans.

The debate about Kennewick's origins was important, because under a law passed in 1990, known as the Native American Graves Protection and Repatriation Act (NAGPRA), Native Americans can reclaim skeletons of Native American ancestry for reburial. When a group of Native Americans (formed of the Umatilla, Colville, Yakama, and Nez Perce tribes) tried to reclaim Kennewick Man, a group of scientists filed a suit to prevent it, claiming that it was an important scientific find and the skeleton needed to be studied. After years of courtroom debate, the scientists were granted three years to conduct studies on the skeleton and those studies are currently under way. If Kennewick was just an isolated case, it might be more of an anomaly, but there are other ancient skeletons that resemble Kennewick, such as Spirit Cave Man from Nevada, and Gordon Creek Woman from Colorado (Owsley and Jantz, 2001).

What does this mean about the ancestry of modern Native Americans and the peopling of North America? First, making conclusions about whole continents of people is difficult to do with a handful of skeletons, so the archaeological record is biased in this sense. Second, it may be that people coming to the Americas did come from multiple areas, but the largest and biggest contributor from Asia eventually became the dominant population in the Americas. Recent genetic data suggest that all modern Native Americans are descended from populations in northern Asia. In any case, it is extremely likely that the debate about Kennewick Man and the origins of Native Americans will continue for a long time to come.

There are many sites that date after Clovis in the Americas. Also called the Paleoindian period (the term used for the earliest people in the Americas), these sites include Folsom, New Mexico; Lindenmeier, Colorado; Gault, Texas; and Daisy Cave, California. All contain stone tool debris and evidence of processing animals for food and hides; some also contain the remains of extinct animals, such as mammoth, mastodon, *Bison antiquus*, and Pleistocene horse. Some researchers have argued that the megafauna in the Americas went extinct at the end of the Pleistocene due to over-hunting by humans (Martin, 1989). Known as the Quaternary Extinction, the period at the end of the Pleistocene ended with over 32 genera of megafauna going extinct in North America alone. This included previously mentioned animals like mammoth, mastodon, *Bison antiquus*, and Pleistocene horse that were hunted by humans (Figure 4-7). But, it also includes animals such as tapir, giant beaver, cave bear, saber-toothed cat, American lion, and dire wolf. The argument that suggests humans were responsible for this extinction event is

Figure 4-7. Mastodon reconstruction.

known as the "Overkill Hypothesis" and indicates that when humans came into the Americas, they came into contact with animals that had never been hunted by humans before, so the animals were easy prey (Martin, 1989). Soon the larger herbivores began to disappear and the predators, such as lions, bears, and cats had no more prey and began to disappear as well. Critics of the overkill hypothesis suggest that it was not humans who were the main factor, but climate change at the end of the Pleistocene (Haynes, 2009). As the climate grew warmer, the larger-bodied animals had trouble adapting and died off. Proponents of the climate change model use other continents (Europe, for example) that had huge quaternary megafaunal die-offs in areas where humans were living for long periods of time. It is probably a combination of both human predation and climate change that caused the extinction of the megafauna. Large mammals reproduce slowly, so with pressure from both human hunting and climate change, it is likely that the megafauna could not reproduce fast enough and eventually died off.

4.3 BRINGING IT TOGETHER

We began this chapter by discussing the spread of humans from Southeast Asia (Sunda) to Australia (Sahul) and learned that boats were necessary for this migration event. By about 50,000 years ago, Australia had been initially colonized with people who hunted and gathered, made stone tools, and created elaborate rock art. We continued looking at migration into the Americas and discovered that there are three different theories for both the timing and the route for the peopling of the Americas. Humans may have come as early as 40,000 years ago and as late as 13,500 years ago into the Americas, but most scholars agree that by about 20,000 years ago there were significant numbers of people coming into the Americas, with perhaps a small, initial colonization as early as 40,000 years ago. Also, humans may have taken three different routes into the Americas: across the Bering Land Bridge, along the Pacific Coast, and across the Atlantic. Again, it is likely that all three routes could have been used, given the evidence from sites, stone tools, and human skeletal remains. Finally, we are seeing the end of the Pleistocene period and its effects on the animals and people around the world. In the next chapter, we will discuss how the global temperatures increased; creating a climate that had shorter winters and longer summers. Also, the increasing temperatures led to the reduction of the ice sheets and higher sea levels. Thus, people who lived around 10,000 years ago were experiencing changes and as we will discuss, cultural changes went hand in hand with these environmental changes.

Key Terms and Concepts

Sunda	Pleistocene land mass that included Southeast Asia and the Indonesia islands.
Sahul	Pleistocene land mass that included Australia, New Guinea, and Tasmania.
Wallacea	The islands between Sunda and Sahul.
Nauwalabila I	The oldest site in Australia, dating between 50,000 and 60,000 years ago.
Lake Mungo	Another ancient site in Australia, dating between 40,000 and 50,000 years ago.

Roonka and Coobool Creek	Australian sites with human burials.
Cranial Deformation	The deliberate alteration of human skulls by binding with cloth.
Gwion Gwion	Area in Australia with rock art, also known as the Bradshaws.
Clovis-first model	Theory for the Peopling of the Americas that suggests people arrived in the Americas no earlier than 13,500 years ago.
Pre-Clovis model	Theory for the Peopling of the Americas that suggests people arrived in the Americas as early as 20,000 years ago.
Early Arrival model	Theory for the Peopling of the Americas that suggests people arrived in the Americas as early as 40,000 years ago.
Meadowcroft Rockshelter, Monte Verde, Cactus Hill	Pre-Clovis era sites.
Pedra Furada, Bluefish Caves	Early Arrival sites.
Blackwater Draw, NM	Clovis First site.
Clovis Point	Large projectile point with flute (or flake) thinning the base.
Bering Land Bridge/Beringia	Pleistocene land mass connecting Siberia and Alaska.
Bering Land Bridge route	Possible route for people coming into the Americas from Siberia, across the land bridge, and into North America.
Pacific Coast route	Theory that people traveled from east Asia, up the Pacific coast, and down into North America.
Atlantic route (Solutrean hypothesis)	Hypothesis that people traveled by boat from Europe to North America.
Soluturean	Type of stone tool found in Europe that is made in a similar way to Clovis points.
Laurentide Ice Sheet	Ice sheet covering middle and eastern Canada and northern U.S.
Cordilleran Ice Sheet	Ice sheet covering the northern Pacific coast.

Kennewick Man	Controversial skeleton found in Washington State that dates to 9,300 years ago and has features that do not resemble modern Native Americans.
Paleoindian	Term used to describe the period of the earliest people in the Americas.
Megafaunal extinction	Phenomenon at the end of the Pleistocene when over 32 mammal genera went extinct.

5: TRANSITION TO FOOD PRODUCERS

5.1 PLANT AND ANIMAL DOMESTICATION

In Chapter 4, we discussed the movement of humans out of Africa, Europe, and Asia and into Australia and the Americas. We also discussed that this migration occurred near the end of the last Ice Age. After the migration of humans to Australia and the Americas, at about 10,000 years ago, the Ice Age gradually ended. This caused changes not only to the climate, with longer summers and warmer winters, but also changed the landscape as sea levels rose due to melting ice sheets. In addition, many of the megafauna, such as mammoth, mastodon, Pleistocene bison, and horses went extinct. Thus, humans had to adjust their settlement and subsistence methods to these changes. In some cases, these adaptations led to the deliberate growing of plants and domestication of animals as a food resource.

It is not as if this transition occurred overnight. Obviously, the temperature and sea level changes were gradual. I think of it as changes based on a generational basis; that is, the grandparents might observe that when they were young, the winters were longer and the summers were shorter. Or, they might have commented that there were more edible plants around than there used to be. In sum, the changes—in some areas of the world—resulted in people relying more on plants to survive, something that was not common in the Ice Age. There are different theories regarding how the domestication of plants and animals came about.

First, however, we need to define what is meant by domestication. Domestication is the deliberate control of the reproduction of plants and animals. In many cases, people practiced artificial selection, which is when plants or animals with certain traits are encouraged to reproduce. For example, if plants grow faster or have larger edible parts, people might

Figure 5-1. Gray Wolves.

Figure 5-2. A Chihuahua (Image by Tyke).

select seeds from those plants to replant. This results in plants and animals that are distinct from their wild counterparts. I like to use the comparison of gray wolves (Figure 5-1) and Chihuahuas (Figure 5-2). All dogs are descended from wolves (most likely wolves from Eurasia), but obviously there was a lot of selection to get from a wolf that weighs around 150 pounds to a three-pound Chihuahua (Morey, 2010).

So how did the domestication process occur? There are two main schools of thought on why humans began to domesticate plants and animals. The first is categorized as the "Pull Model" and contends that the environment changed and plants grew better and animals reproduced more, so people were "pulled" into domestication. This concept works particularly well when trying to explain the domestication of plants. We know that the environment warmed considerably at the end of the Ice Age and warmer environments are conducive to plant growth. Humans became increasingly familiar with plants and animals around them and began to domesticate them. Humans could have also unintentionally promoted dispersal of certain types of plants by weeding, storing, and irrigating particular wild resources. As these plants became more common, reliance on them increased. People also may have became more tethered to their territories to encourage the growth of the plants and become more sedentary.

Another model, known as the "Push Model," suggests that people were pushed into domestication when the climate changed. In this model, the hypothesis is that societies intensified food production only when forced to by population pressure on resources. For example, it is possible that when sea levels rose, coastal people moved inland and this led to population pressure on groups already there, so people needed to intensify food production to get enough food for their families. Human populations had spread to all areas of the world, and they used all the available food resources, so continued population growth resulted in the need to produce more food.

While it is tempting to find one clear reason for people to change their way of living, it is probably a combination of both: a better climate for plant growth and an increase in human population. The key to domestication is that it increases the amount of food produced per acre. There are some sacrifices in nutrition, however, because the variety of food consumed is reduced, but the production is increased and it creates food surpluses. These plant foods and meats can be processed and preserved for use during the winter months and to help if there is drought or disease that affects the food supply. Also, the surplus food can be traded for other things that are not locally available. Another aspect is because there are surpluses, not everyone needs to work for food. Some people who are good at other things can use those skills to trade for food. People can develop their skills and so we see an increase in the complexity of all kinds of activities.

We will explore the social changes that took place with the advent of plant and animal domestication later in this chapter and in subsequent chapters. Right now, many of you might be thinking, what might have been some of the earliest domesticates? Or, you might be thinking, why were some plants and animals domesticated and others were not? Some scholars have come up with criteria to help understand what characteristics wild plants and animals had that made them more conducive to domestication (Diamond, 1999).

Plants selected for domestication have several traits that make them conducive to being grown by humans. One trait is that they germinate quickly; that is, they grow quickly once they are spread from the parent plant. In addition, plants should have predictable germination and growth, so that people know when to plant the seeds and now how long it will take them to grow from seeds to adult plants. The seeds of domesticated plants should also adhere to the plant for a longer period of time, so that they can be harvested all at once. There should also be fewer defenses, such as spines or plant secretions to ward off insects. Finally, plants chosen for domestication should have the capability to grow larger edible parts, such as seeds, fruits, or roots, so that humans can get the most for the amount of energy they put into tending the plants.

Animals selected for domestication have at least four main characteristics that are usually present (Diamond, 1999). First, they should have a flexible diet; animals that will eat a variety of foods are easier to tend. For example, herbivores that will eat grass are less expensive to keep. Two other criteria are to have a good rate of growth and easy reproduction. The more quickly an animal can grow means they can be harvested for meat and hides, or used for animal byproducts such as milk and blood. Reproducing quickly can increase herds and also certain traits can more easily be selected for by breeders. Animals should have a social disposition. Some of the animals domesticated could be very aggressive, such as wolves, wild boars, and aurochs. But, all of these animals have a social hierarchy and if humans can assert themselves to become, essentially, the leader of the pack, they can control the animals and select for less aggressive animals as they breed them. Scholars also think that animals with calm temperaments are easier to keep in captivity. Some animals, such as domestic sheep, still have a strong tendency to panic, but most sheep also flock, so they stay together and thus can be herded by people and dogs.

How do we recognize domestic plants and animals archaeologically? This can be harder than you might think. Because the change over time is so gradual, there is a long time between when physical differences might appear between wild plants and animals and their domestic counterparts. For plants, as mentioned briefly above, we see seeds more securely attached to the plant. This is very different from wild plants, which lose their seeds gradually, thus increasing the chance that some of the seeds will avoid being eaten and germinate. Also, plants that have larger edible parts over time are an indication of domestication. Finally, finding plants outside their native area means the seeds are being traded for goods or services and then grown in new areas.

Early animal domestication can be recognized through various changes. In general, initial domesticates are smaller than their wild counterparts. This may have been to make them more manageable. Also, if animals have horns, such as cattle, sheep, and goats, those horns become much smaller. It is likely that members of a herd with smaller size and smaller horns were selected to be bred for better herding and management. We also start to see cultural changes, with both plants and animals. For example, we see particular plants and animals in artwork and buried with the dead. Finally, we see animals outside their native areas, such as horses (which were originally domesticated in Eurasia) in Egypt.

Where different plants and animals were first domesticated is also an important issue. For plants, the earliest domestication occurred in the Near East, in the area that today is Israel, Syria, and Iraq. Figs, barley, and wheat all were domesticated in this region. Another area with very early plants is Asia, where we have bottle gourds and rice. Bottle gourds were likely used as containers rather than food. From the Americas, the earliest domesticates are potatoes, beans, squash, and maize. Most people are very surprised to hear that potatoes were first domesticated in the Andes Mountains of South America, because we typically associate potatoes with Irish food. In fact, potatoes were not introduced to Ireland until the 16th century. Early African domesticates include sorghum and millet. Plants could either be cooked and consumed (such as potatoes, corn, beans, and rice) or processed into flour and made into flat bread or mixed with other foods.

Animals were domesticated all over the world for a variety of reasons. The earliest animal to be domesticated was the dog, which was domesticated from the Eurasian wolf as early as 30,000 years ago (Vila et al., 1997). Dogs were probably used to help in hunting, as well as for protection, pack carrying, and companions (Morey, 2010). Sheep and goats were also domesticated early and were used for meat, milk, and wool. Cattle also had a variety of uses, including for milk, hides, and meat, but they could also pull plows to till fields. Similarly, water buffalo were used for plowing rice fields in Asia. Llamas and alpacas were primarily used for carrying packs in South America, but their wool was also used. Birds, such as chickens, ducks, geese, and turkeys provided meat, feathers, and eggs. Camels and horses were used for transporting people and goods, but also provided meat and milk.

5.2. DOG DOMESTICATION

Dogs are unique compared to other animal domesticates for several reasons. First, they were the earliest animal to be domesticated. Second, they are the most geographically widespread of any domesticate. Third, they served humans in a wide array of capacities, including hunting, pack carrying, food, and companions. Fourth, we also see dogs in spiritual situations, such as buried with humans or in the same cemeteries as humans. Thus, dogs were involved in every facet of human life.

Currently, the earliest dog remains come from Siberia (Ovodov et al., 2011), Belgium, and the Ukraine (Germonpre et al., 2008). The dogs from these sites date to over 30,000 years ago. Earlier, we explored some characteristics that animals have to have to be conducive to domestication, including flexible diet, good growth rate and reproduction, social disposition, and calm temperaments. Wolves have all of those characteristics, even though calm temperaments may not be the first thing we think of when we think about wolves. So, how did dogs become domesticated from wolves? One theory is that people took in wolf pups and raised them; then, they bred these pups for certain traits, so that they eventually became different from their wild counterparts (Morey, 2010). Another theory is that some wolves may have been attracted to human camps. These dogs may have lost their fear of humans and interacted with them, then gradually bred and reproduced with each other. Some scholars think these dogs might have been the more subordinate in wolf packs and subordinate traits may have helped humans manage and train them.

While it is difficult to document archaeologically, we know from ethnohistoric documents that dogs were used to help humans hunt. They would be able to track down prey and keep it at bay until humans arrived. They could also bring down smaller prey to either feed themselves or share with their human caregivers. Examinations of dog remains from some archaeological sites have also shown that dogs may have carried packs or pulled sleds for humans. The remains had damage to the vertebra of the upper pack, which was most probably due to consistently bearing weight (Walker et al., 2005). Before horses were domesticated, and in the New World where horses were not reintroduced until the 1600s, the ability to have dogs carry items from one place to another would have been a valuable asset. Dogs could also have served humans as guard dogs, camp "cleaners" (cleaning up food refuse), and companions.

Figure 5-3. Dog burial from Dust Cave, Alabama (modified from Walker et al. 2005).

One of the most interesting aspects of the relationship between dogs and humans is that humans buried their dogs in the same cemeteries and sometimes the same graves as their loved ones.

Burying dogs dates back to at least 10,000 years ago in Siberia (Morey, 2005). Other early dog burials are from the Americas and date to 8,500 years ago (Morey and Wiant, 1992). In some cases there are just a few dogs in the cemeteries, such as at the site of Dust Cave in Alabama (Figure 5-3), where there are four dogs buried (Walker et al., 2005). Conversely, at the site of Ashkelon in Israel there are thousands of dogs buried in a cemetery adjacent to an equally large human cemetery.

The phenomenon of burying dogs with humans reveals that they did not just serve a secular role for humans, but also a sacred role. Dogs may have been guardians or spirit guides for the dead (Morey, 2010). In some cases, such as at the Indian Knoll and Spirit Hill sites in the Americas, dogs were buried in a protective or guarding pose. For example, at Indian Knoll, a dog was curled around the head of a child (Webb, 1946) and at the Spirit Hill site, one dog was buried on the lap of a human individual and another was placed on the chest of a human (Walker and Windham, n.d.). The burials of dogs and humans indicate that dogs served a sacred role in human society, as well as secular roles.

5.3 EURASIAN STEPPE PASTORALISTS

Throughout the world, there have been animals that people depended on for food, transportation, and trade. But, in some areas, people relied more heavily on animals than on plants. In Eurasian, for example, the horse herders of the Steppe region were famous for crossing great distances for trade, but also building elaborate tombs for their dead.

This culture, also known as the Pazyryk, lived in what is today Siberia and the Ukraine between 2,600 and 2,300 years ago, but also traveled as far as India, China, and Eastern Europe for trade. They were highly nomadic and bred horses that were renowned for their beauty, speed, and stamina. The remains of Pazyryk horses have been recovered from outside burial tombs, where they were sacrificed to be buried with humans entombed in inner chambers. The horses often had beautiful wool saddles, bridles, and headdresses buried with them (Figure 5-4). In a study by Gala Argent, ten horses from a tomb in southern Siberian were studied to determine their age and the elaborateness of their saddles and headdresses (2010). Argent found that the younger horses (aged from 10–11) had more simple saddles with leather fringe, slightly older horses (aged from 9–17) had saddles with pendants and more elaborate appliqués, and the two oldest horses (aged 18 and 20) had longer pendants on the saddles with detailed appliqués, and both were buried with headdresses shaped like antlers. Argent concludes that, while the horses were important for accompanying the deceased into the afterlife, each horse had an important role given their age and experience. In addition to trading the horses, the Pazyryk could also have consumed horse meat as well as milk and butter.

Some of the tombs of the Pazyryk (also known as kurgans) have been found incredibly well preserved, because they are placed in areas where permafrost freezes the remains and the freezing temperature keeps the organic remains from decaying. The more

Figure 5-4. Pazyryk horseman.

Figure 5-5. Mummy of the "Siberian Ice Maiden".

elaborate tombs are of people who had higher status in society and may have been shamans or chiefs. Most of the tombs contain adult males, but a few with women have also been found. One tomb with an adult male is known as "The Chief," because he was found with multiple weapons. The Chief's remains were well preserved not only because the permafrost had frozen the body, but also because the body was mummified. Pazyryk burial ritual includes removing the skin, muscles, and organs from deceased individuals and then sewing the skin back onto the skeletons with horse hair. The Pazyryk were also famous for the elaborate tattoos on their shamans and priests, which often depicted deer stags with elaborate antlers or goats with large, curled horns.

Another Pazyryk burial is known as the "Siberian Ice Maiden" and was found in 1993 by Natalia Polosmak (van Noten and Polosmak, 1995). It is rare, because it is the only kurgan excavated so far that contains a single woman. Inside the Ice Maiden's tomb was a large, larch tree coffin that contained her remains as well as a three-foot-long headdress. She was mummified and buried with her clothing that included a woolen skirt and leggings and a silk blouse. Studies of the silk indicated that the silk was from undomesticated silk worms and so probably came from India. The kurgan also contained two small wooden tables, horsemeat, and a horn cup. Like the burial of the chief, she had elaborate tattoos that were located on her shoulder, wrist, and thumb (Figure 5-5). Six horses were buried outside of her tomb and were killed by being hit on the head.

The Pazyryk were highly nomadic pastoralists, meaning they moved around a lot and had large territories. However, pastoralists, like those found in East Africa, were more territorial and practiced a type of pastoralism known as transhumance. Transhumance is the seasonal movement of animals to different pastures and often only a portion of the group travels with the herds when they move to pastures that are away from their villages. In East Africa, the movement of the herds is predicated by seasonal patterns of rainfall. In general, young men will move with the herds to take advantage of rainfall in other areas and the women, children, and older men will stay behind in the village.

5.4 BRINGING IT TOGETHER

In this chapter, we discussed the beginning of plant and animal domestication. We also discussed the possible reasons domestication occurred, including environmental and population factors. Plants were domesticated as early as 11,000 years ago in the Middle East, with other areas following soon after. Plants may have been domesticated because, after the Ice Age ended and the climate warmed, plants grew better and people began to rely on them more. Or, the human population may have increased due to better climate and they had to increase the amount of food in the environment by domesticating plants. The earliest domestic animal is the dog, domesticated as early as 30,000 years ago in Eurasia. Animals may have been domesticated in a variety of ways, from the deliberate capture of wild animals for breeding, or some animals (such as wolves) could have gradually lost their fear of humans and been easier to control. Sheep and goats were the next to be domesticated around the end of the last Ice Age. We also discussed pastoralists such as the Pazyryk and how some people relied much more on animals to make a living, rather than on plants. We will discuss agriculturalists, or people who mostly rely on plants, more in subsequent chapters.

Key Terms and Concepts

Domestication	The process of deliberate control over the reproduction of wild plants and animals, so that they eventually become new species.
Pull Model	The theory of domestication that suggests environmental changes caused people to domesticate plants.
Ashkelon, Israel	Large cemetary site with over a thousand dog burials.
Dust Cave, Indian Knoll, Spirit Hill	Sites in North America with domestic dog burials.
Push Model	The theory of domestication that argues it was the increase in human population at the end of the Ice Age that induced people to domesticate plants.
Pazyryk	People who had domestic horses and lived on the Eurasian steppes between 2,600 and 2,300 years ago.
Kurgan	Burial mound of the Pazyryk people, containing mummified humans, artifacts, and sacrificed horses.
"The Chief"	Pazyryk burial of an adult male with elaborate tattoos and burial artifacts.
"The Siberian Ice Maiden"	Burial of an adult Pazyryk woman, buried with an elaborate horse hair headdress, silk and wool clothing, and sacrificed horses.

6: EARLY AGRICULTURAL SOCIETIES

6.1 FERTILE CRESCENT

In this chapter, we will be discovering how agricultural societies became increasingly complex. As we have discussed, the end of the Ice Age and the beginning of the Holocene epoch (our current geologic epoch) marked major changes for humans. In some areas of the world, this meant the domestication of plants and animals. We discussed in Chapter 5 how domestication occurred in a variety of places and at different times. The earliest domestication of plants occurred in the Middle East, in an area known as the "Fertile Crescent". Eventually, we start to see early towns and greater social stratification. We will also examine the development of agriculture in Europe. Finally, we will learn about the construction of public structures that are used for a variety of purposes.

The Fertile Crescent extends today from Israel and Jordan in the south, up into Turkey, Syria, and Lebanon in the north, and east into northern Iraq and western Iran (Figure 6-1). It is an area of Mediterranean climate characterized by dry summers and winter rains. There is enough precipitation to support vegetation ranging from woodlands to open park woodland. People inhabiting the area prior to agriculture were known as the Kebarans and they hunted wild game and gathered wild plants. They made composite tools of bone or antler embedded with blades to create projectile points, knives, and scrapers. Kent Flannery has called this period a "Broad-Spectrum Revolution" and theorized that new hunting strategies were developed that focused on small game, while still supplementing their diet

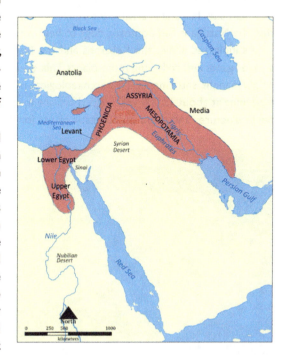

Figure 6-1. Map of the Fertile Crescent (Image by Nafsadh).

with meat from wild herd animals like gazelle, goats, and sheep (1969). The focus on small game and increased use of plants would have meant they could stay in one place longer and probably set the stage for sedentism (living in one place year round).

The Kebarans thrived in the Fertile Crescent from about 20,000 to 14,000 years ago. Following this, we see even more dependence on small game and plants with the Natufian culture. However, the Natufians continued to hunt gazelle when available and depended heavily on wild cereal grasses. They also used blades (or even small bladelets) to create composite tools of antler handles with blades imbedded in them. In addition, we see an increase in the use of ground stone tools (tools for grinding and processing plant remains) that supports the importance of plants in their diet. The Natufians were semi-sedentary and built small villages containing domestic structures.

Ain Mallaha, which was a Natufian village that settled around 14,000 years ago in what is today Israel, had multiple structures (Chazan, 2011). The houses were semi-subterranean, with subterranean floors and stone walls. It is probable that wooden posts were thatched (woven with grasses) to form the walls and roof of the structures. There were also fire pits for cooking, heat, and light located inside the structures. Around a dozen structures were discovered and whole families lived in these one-room houses. It is difficult to estimate the total population, but if families had 3–5 children and grandparents living with them, then the settlement was probably home to around one hundred people.

The burial of individuals upon death was in the floors of abandoned houses. It may be that whole families were buried in the floors of houses that were abandoned. In one site, one house had over 10 people buried in the floor and in another, a dozen people were found. Some of the individuals buried at Ain Mallaha were wearing jewelry made out of shells, perforated animal teeth, and stone beads. In one of the houses, an individual was buried in a fetal position on their right side, with their left hand covering the remains of puppy. At another Natufian site, Hayonim Terrace, the remains of a human were found buried with a dog. This probably indicates that the Natufians had domestic dogs to help with hunting, carrying wood or meat, and as camp guards.

As indicated above, the Kebarans and the Natufians developed subsistence strategies that included hunting smaller game and collecting more plants. This eventually led to the domestication of plants and the development of permanent settlements. This archaeological period is known as the Neolithic period (or New Stone Age). Beginning at about 12,000 years ago, there are multiple settlements across the Fertile Crescent that have permanent structures and relied on domestic plants for their subsistence. Technology also changed at this time and we see a reliance on blades that are used for sickles to cut plants and small arrowheads made from blades.

It is likely that there was not a lot of social stratification at early Neolithic sites. We do not see a lot of differences in the burials or structures that would indicate some people had higher status over others. However, we do know that settlement size increased during this period and we see the first evidence of communal structures. Prior to this, all structures served a domestic purpose, which means they were used by individual families for living, cooking, sleeping, and other activities. At some of the early Neolithic sites, we start to see communal or public structures, which were used by the whole

Figure 6-2. House foundations at Jericho.

community. This generally indicates a higher level of stratification, such as when a leader needs to address a group people might be called to a communal structure.

The famous biblical city of Jericho epitomizes the early Neolithic village with many family structures as well as communal structures (Scarre, 2005). It is located in what is today Palestine, approximately nine miles from the Dead Sea. Occupied as early as 11,000 years ago, Jericho is one of the oldest continuously occupied cities in the world (Figure 6-2). The initial occupation consisted of small circular houses, the burial of the dead in building floors (similar to the Natufian site of Ain Mallaha), and the use of communal structures (Kenyon, 1967). The people of Jericho hunted wild animals, such as gazelle, wild goats, and sheep, and cultivated plants, such as emmer wheat, barley, and rye. However, unlike later Neolithic sites, the people of Jericho did not have pottery jars for storing food or cooking, so sometimes early Neolithic sites like Jericho are referred to as "Pre-Pottery Neolithic."

Jericho was contained within a wall made of stone and mud brick. This wall had a tower that was over 30 feet high, also made of stone and mud brick, and attached to the inside of the wall. It is thought to have been used as a defensive structure. Defensive structures become increasingly common in the Neolithic, because groups had territories and crops to defend. The wall enclosed only the residential houses and public structures, so if raids occurred when people were out in their fields, they would have to retreat to the city center for protection.

Other early Neolithic cities include Abu Hureyra and Jerf el Ahmar, both located in Syria. Abu Hureyra was occupied around 11,000 years ago and was a city made up of mud brick houses. Examination of the human remains from the site shows that there was probably heavy agricultural labor, due to pathologies on the skeleton associated with field labor and plant processing. In particular, the skeletons of human females often had enlarged tibiae (shin bones) and toes that were bent upwards (Molleson, 1994). This suggests women kneeling for extended periods of time. The women also had signs of wear and tear on their lower backs and elbows.

At the site of Jerf el Ahmar there is evidence of continuous occupation throughout the Neolithic. Jerf el Ahmar is also an example of a "tell," which is when cities are built on top of each other in the same place, resulting in a human-made hill. In the case of Jerf el Ahmar, there were at least 10 different rebuilding episodes. Excavations recovered thousands of charred plant fragments, with barley predominating. Also recovered were several hundred grinding stones, suggesting plant processing zones (Moore et al., 2001).

Another famous southwest Asian Neolithic site is Çatalhöyük, Turkey. The population of the site is estimated to be 5,000 and the inhabitants lived in mud brick houses, similar to the ones found at Abu Hureyra and Jerf el Ahmar (Hodder, 2006). The houses in Çatalhöyük were accessed by the roof, with ladders leading to the interior. There are not streets or alleys at the site, so people probably traveled from one house to another via the rooftops. The interiors of the houses were plastered and sometimes painted with elaborate murals featuring people and animals. Smaller storage rooms were often located near a main room and the main room was for all activities, such as food preparation, cooking, eating, and sleeping. Also similar to Abu Hureyra and Jerf el Ahmar, the deceased were buried in the floors of the houses. In some cases, the heads were removed from the skeleton, plastered, and placed in niches in the walls. These heads may have been used in mourning or ancestor rituals. In addition to human

Figure 6-3. Interior house reconstruction at Çatalhöyük featuring bull heads (Image by Georges Jansoone).

heads, the heads of animals were also mounted on the walls. Cattle, in particular, are featured, with particular emphasis on the horns of the animals (Figure 6-3).

Also similar to other Neolithic sites, Çatalhöyük does not appear to have differences between people based on social status. The houses are similar in size and decoration and the deceased individuals generally receive similar treatment (burial in floors). The treatment of the heads of some of the deceased does suggest some ancestor worship, however. In addition, there are several examples of female figurines, with the most studied being the "Seated Goddess" showing a female sitting on a large chair that is flanked by two lion figures. Initially, excavators thought the female figures represented a goddess cult (Mellart, 1967), but excavations in the 1990s recovered more figures and most were of animals (Hodder, 2006). It is most likely that people and animals were important to the lives of the Jericho inhabitants were depicted as figurines and in murals.

6.2 MESOLITHIC AND NEOLITHIC EUROPE

The site of Star Carr in Great Britain, is an important Mesolithic site. The Mesolithic period predates the Neolithic, but we see the development of semi-sedentary settlements that probably led to sedentary settlements and the development of agriculture, which are hallmarks of the Neolithic period. Star Carr was located in a bog in Yorkshire, England, and was discovered in 1947 by John Moore (Clark, 1954). Multiple excavations revealed that the site was first occupied around 9,500 years ago by a small group of hunter-gatherers. Materials collected at the site include stone axes and adzes that were probably used to clear land, bone and antler spear points for hunting, and stone tools for hunting and processing food. Animal remains recovered from the site indicate that red deer (elk), aurochs (wild cattle), and roe deer were the main prey species. The presence of dog remains at the site suggests that dogs may have been used to track and hunt these animals.

The most striking thing about Star Carr is the preservation of organic remains. As stated above, faunal remains and bone artifacts were recovered in abundance. In addition, 21 headdresses of red deer antler and skull were recovered (Figure 6-4). These are unique in the archaeological record and some researchers have suggested they were used for ceremonial purposes and others have argued that they were used in hunting red deer to make stalking them easier (Legg and Rowley-Conwy, 1988; Scarre, 2005). It may be that they were used for both purposes: rituals to invoke sympathetic magic for a successful hunt and using the headdresses and perhaps hides of the animals to provide camouflage during the hunt.

Excavations during the last 12 years have provided more finds, such as the possible "earliest" structure in England (Conneller, 2007). Re-excavation of work done by Clark has unfortunately revealed that the bog is shrinking and the acidity of the bog is increasing. This means that the excellent organic preservation that the site is known for is becoming compromised. Bone is becoming weak and "rubbery" and wood is falling apart as soon as it is excavated (Star Carr Archaeology Project). It is unclear yet why these conditions have changed and researchers from the University of York are working to find ways to stabilize this unique site.

Figure 6-4. Red deer antler and skull headdress from Star Carr.

While Star Carr represents a hunting and gathering society in Great Britain, the size of the site and the manipulation of the environment suggest that people were becoming more tethered to the landscape. By 6,000 years ago much of Europe was farming, with permanent houses and domestic animals. Evidence of this life way can be found at Skara Brae, located in Orkney, Scotland. It is a large settlement that contains the remains of ten houses. The houses are extremely well made and contain furniture composed of stone and stone-lined hearths (Figure 6-6). Materials from in and around the houses suggest that people farmed

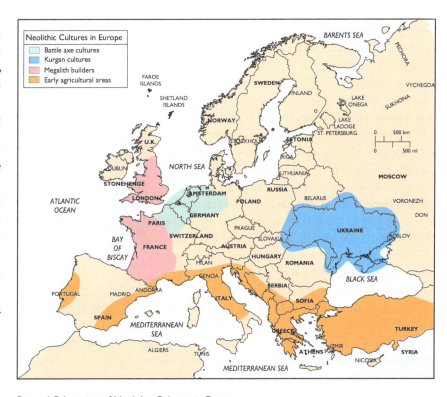

Figure 6-5. Location of Neolithic Cultures in Europe.

barley and raised sheep and cattle (Laing, 1974). Fish and shellfish supplemented the diet and kelp (sea weed) found in the hearths suggests that this was used as fuel (Fenton, 1978). They also made pottery, in a style known as "grooved ware," which was a pot with a flat bottom, straight sides, and grooved decorations on the rim.

Other evidence for Neolithic life ways in Europe can be inferred from the body of a man found by hikers in the Alps in 1991. The body was initially suspected to be from a recent hiker who died while out climbing, however, radiocarbon analysis revealed that he died over 5,000 years ago. Named "Ötzi" after the Ötztaler region of the Alps where he was found, Ötzi was perfectly preserved in a constantly cold environment, thus preserving his skin, muscles, internal organs, as well as the clothing and gear he had with him when he died. Subsequent analyses of his remains indicate that he was from or had recently visited an agricultural village, where he consumed a last meal of roasted goat and einkorn wheat (Bortenschlager and Oeggl, 2000). At the time of death, he was approximately five-and-a-half feet tall and around 45 years old (Fowler, 2000).

The materials found with Ötzi indicate that he was well equipped for the cold climate, with warm clothing, weapons, and a "first aid kit" of fungi and mosses known to have medicinal uses (Fowler, 2000). His clothing consisted of a woven grass cloak, a bearskin hat, leather leggings, and shoes stuffed

Figure 6-6. Remains of a house structure at Skara Brae, Scotland (Image by John Burka).

with grass. In addition, he carried a copper axe complete with handle, two bark baskets, a flint knife, a bow, and a quiver with 14 arrows. Despite being so well equipped, Ötzi died high in the Alps after a violent altercation with other individuals. He had defensive wounds on his arms and hands, suggesting a struggle with someone armed with a knife. A CAT scan done in 2001 revealed an arrow imbedded in his left shoulder. The arrow entered from his back and the shaft was removed, indicating that someone tried to remove the arrow, possibly in an attempt to save his life or to remove the evidence of the cause of his death. Unfortunately, it is likely that the arrow caused blood loss and his eventual death. However, recent research suggests that a blow to the head was the main cause of death (Nerlich et al., 2009).

Figure 6-7. West Kennet Long Barrow.

Ötzi's remains provide unique insight into what life was like in the Neolithic. Certainly, not everyone at that time met a violent end, but agricultural life means that there are increased demands to protect territories for growing crops and sedentary villages. Interpersonal conflict increases tremendously in the Neolithic and subsequent periods. Ötzi is also unique, because his remains were not preserved in a formal burial setting. All evidence indicates an accidental death and abandonment, after which his remains were covered with snow and ice and preserved for 5,000 years. His clothing and gear reflect everyday wear and equipment, thus giving us a picture of what common Neolithic people wore and carried with them, rather than the sometimes more elaborate style of a formal burial.

Another important aspect of Neolithic life is the appearance of monuments of standing stones, with the earliest stone monuments in Europe dating to around 5,000–6,000 years ago. Megaliths are prehistoric monuments made of large stones. In general, the structures can be divided into three categories, including tumuli (a mound of earth, grass, and stones that covers a tomb), menhirs (the upright or standing stones; standing stones are often arranged in circles or lines), and dolmens (three or more upright stones with a stone that balances on top).

All three types of monuments are found in Great Britain. Tumulus mounds appear around 6,000 years ago and some notable sites include West Kennet Long Barrow, Wayland's Smithy, Belas Knap, Maeshowe, and Duggleby Howe. West Kennet Long Barrow, located in Wiltshire, England, has two pairs of opposing stone chambers and a single interior chamber used for burial (Figure 6-7). A total of 46 individuals were interred in the barrow. The age of the individuals ranges from infants to the elderly of both sexes, though one chamber contained a majority of juveniles and another mostly men (Pollard, 2008). Belas Knap, another well-known long barrow site, is located in Gloucestershire, England. The barrow is about 178 feet long, 60 feet wide, and 14 feet high (Pollard, 2008). Forty-four skeletons were recovered from the site, along with animal remains and broken pottery. Like West Kennet Long Barrow, as well as the other barrows previously mentioned, Belas Knap is located on a pronounced hilltop. The site may have served a function as a territorial marker or gathering space in addition to a burial ground.

Avebury is an example of a menhir, or standing stones arranged in a circle. Thus, it is a true henge. Currently, the site consists of a grass-covered bank approximately 1,300 feet in diameter and 20 feet high with a deep inner ditch. The ditch has four entrances pointing to the cardinal compass points. Inside the ditch is a circle of large stones enclosing approximately 28 acres of land. This circle, originally composed of at least 98 stones but now having only 27, encloses two smaller stone circles, each being about 340 feet in diameter. The two inner circles are believed to have been constructed first, around 4,600 years ago, while the large outer ring and earthwork

Figure 6-8. Stonehenge as seen today.

date from 4,500 years ago. The construction of the Avebury complex must have required enormous efforts on the part of the local inhabitants. The sarsen stones, ranging in height from nine to over 20 feet and weighing as much as 40 tons, were first carved from bedrock and then dragged or sledded a distance of nearly two miles from their quarry site. The excavation of the encircling ditch required an estimated 200,000 tons of rock to be chipped and scraped away with wooden shovels, and stone and antler picks.

Probably the most famous Neolithic site on the Salisbury Plains in Great Britain is Stonehenge. This site was built in three different periods. In Period I (radiocarbon-dated to 5,100 years ago), Stonehenge was a circular ditch with an internal bank. The circle, 320 feet in diameter, had a single entrance, 56 mysterious holes around its perimeter (with remains of human cremations in them), and a wooden sanctuary in the middle. The circle was aligned with the midsummer sunrise, the midwinter sunset, and the most southerly rising and northerly setting of the moon (Chazan, 2011). Period II (4,150 years ago) saw the replacement of the wooden sanctuary with two circles of "bluestones" (dolerite stone with a bluish tint), the widening of the entrance, the construction of an entrance avenue marked by parallel ditches aligned to the midsummer sunrise, and the erection, outside the circle, of the thirty-five-ton "Heel Stone." The eighty bluestones, some weighing as much as four tons, were transported from the Prescelly Mountains in Wales, 240 miles away. During Period III (4,075 years ago), the bluestones were taken down and the enormous "sarsen" stones were erected (Figure 6-8). These stones, averaging eighteen feet in height and weighing twenty-five tons, were transported from near the Avebury stone rings twenty miles to the north. Sometime between 3,500 and 3,100 years ago, sixty of the bluestones were reset in a circle immediately inside the sarsen circle, and another nineteen were placed in a horseshoe pattern, also inside the circle.

It has been estimated that the three phases of the construction required more than thirty million hours of labor. It is unlikely that Stonehenge was functioning much after 3,000 years ago, but the area continued to be utilized, as is evidence by Bronze Age tumulus burials on the hilltops surrounding the site. Although much work has focused on the standing stones, recent excavations have documented a large settlement around the site. This settlement may have been occupied during certain times of the year, when people traveled to Stonehenge for ceremonies or events.

There are many theories regarding the function of Stonehenge. The presence of cremated remains in the Aubrey holes suggests a burial ground. The site may also have been used to identify ancient trade routes or territories. There are many Neolithic villages in the vicinity of Stonehenge and, as we have discussed, territory becomes an important commodity during Neolithic times. Other theories are that the site served as a center for worship and religious ceremonies. It is often assumed that the large amount of work involved in building a monument of this kind required some binding principle or impetus. Religion served the function of organizing people and bringing them together, so this may have been an important factor in the construction of Stonehenge. Finally, Stonehenge may have served as an astronomical observatory, due to the clearly documented alignment of Stonehenge with astronomical events. During the summer solstice, the sun shines past the heel stone and lights up the center dolmens. Although Stonehenge has often been cited as a place that was frequently visited during the summer solstice and may relate to celebration of the longest day of the year and, perhaps, the season of planting crops, recent evidence suggests the site was most frequently visited during the winter solstice. This has been suggested due to the existence of other megalithic monuments (Newgrange and Maeshowe) that face the winter solstice sunrise. Also, recent excavations in the surrounding area indicate no occupation during the summer months (Pollard, 2008). Whatever the function of Stonehenge, it stands as testament to the ability of Neolithic people to organize for large-scale labor, shows a great understanding of the cycles of the sun and other astronomical events, and reveals a strong tie to place on the Neolithic landscape.

6.3. BRINGING IT TOGETHER

In Chapter 6, we have seen the development of agriculture in several key regions of the world. The earliest agricultural probably developed in the Fertile Crescent, or Middle Eastern, part of the world. The earliest cultigens include wheat, millet, barley, and rice. We also learned about the earliest permanent settlements, such as Ain Mallaha and Jericho where people lived in communities with many domestic structures and some (like Jericho) were fortified for protection. As people become more sedentary, they also become more complex in terms of craft specialization (particularly pottery), settlements, burials, and social structure. In addition, we see the development of public architecture as is evidenced by some of the Neolithic megaliths of Europe. These megalithic structures were typically constructed and reconstructed over many centuries, took tremendous effort and knowledge to build and sometimes contained material that came from many miles away. It is clear that the Neolithic period brought about vast change in human societies and, as we will see in subsequent chapters, human complexity and innovation continues to change in many areas of the world.

Key Terms and Concepts

Fertile Crescent	An area of early agricultural development that extends today from Israel and Jordan in the south, up into Turkey, Syria, and Lebanon in the north, and east into northern Iraq and western Iran.
"Broad-Spectrum Revolution"	A theory by Kent Flannery, who theorized that new hunting strategies were developed in the Holocene that focused on small game, while still supplementing their diet with meat from herd animals like gazelle, goats, and sheep.
Kebarans	People inhabiting the Fertile Crescent prior to agriculture and hunted wild game and gathered wild plants.
Natufians	A culture living in the Fertile Crescent that depended heavily on wild cereal grasses, which eventually gave rise to the early domesticates, such as wheat, barley, and rye.

Ain Mallaha	Settled around 14,000 years ago in what is today Israel, contained multiple structures and evidence of early farming.
Jericho	An early Neolithic village with many structures, it is located in what is today Palestine, approximately 15 kilometers from the Dead Sea. Occupied as early as 11,000 years ago, Jericho is one of the oldest continuously occupied cities in the world.
Abu Hureya and Jerh al Ahmar	Sites in the Fertile Crescent, occupied around 9,000 BC and contained mud brick houses.
Çatalhöyük	A Neolithic site in Turkey. The population of the site is estimated to be 5,000 and the inhabitants lived in mud brick houses accessed through the roof. Elaborate burial rituals and decorated houses are indicative of complex social structure.
Star Carr	Located in a bog in Yorkshire, England, excavations revealed that the site was first occupied around 9,500 years ago by a small group of hunter-gatherers. Elk headdresses were discovered at the site.
Skara Brae	Located in Orkney, Scotland. It is a large settlement that contains the remains of ten houses that contain furniture composed of stone as well as stone-lined hearths.
West Kennet Long Barrow and Belas Knap	"Long barrow" or burial sites in Neolithic Great Britain.
Megaliths	Large Neolithic monuments of standing stones.
Averbury and Stonehenge, England	Large megalithic structures.

7: MESOPOTAMIA

7.1 SUMERIA

In Chapter 6, we discussed some areas of the world that developed agriculture and social complexity. In this chapter, we will explore the increasing social complexity in Mesopotamia. Mesopotamia is located in the Tigris and Euphrates river valleys, which his in the current countries of Iraq, Syria, and Turkey. Mesopotamia is home to the earliest civilization in the world and some of the oldest cities. The natural resources in the area were probably why agriculture and social complexity evolved. Specifically, the land is fertile due to seasonal rains that flooded the river valleys. The river valleys also had marshy areas with wide, flat plains that were good for agriculture. As population increased due to surplus food from agriculture, cities developed along the rivers.

So, what were these early civilizations and cities like? One of the earliest cities from this area is Uruk, located along the Euphrates River and established around 6,000 years ago. At the height of its development, the city covered almost four square miles, had a wall around much of the city center, and housed around 60,000 people (Liverani et al., 2006). The city was composed of several districts, some were residential and some contained public structures and monuments. The early public structures are significant because they represent

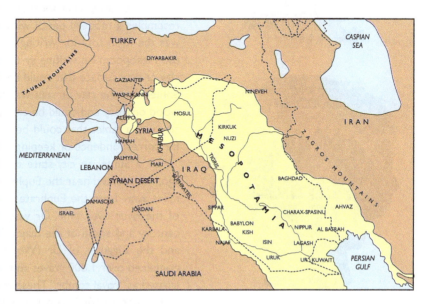

Figure 7-1.

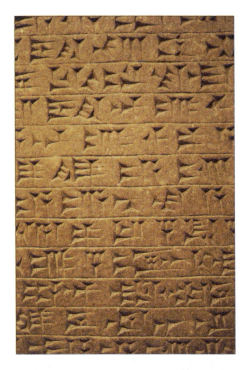

Figure 7-2. Close up of a cuneiform tablet (Image by Matt Neale).

Figure 7-3. Gold headdress buried with Queen Puabi in the Royal Tombs of Ur

community gathering places and areas for government offices and royal palaces. One of these public structures includes the Ziggurat of Inanna. A ziggurat is a large structure, made of mud brick and stone, that was used for religious rituals (Crawford, 1993). Inanna is the Mesopotamian goddess of love, fertility, and warfare and offerings were made to her at this ziggurat. Another ziggurat in Uruk was the Ziggurat of Anu used for worship of the god Anu. Anu was the god of heaven, the sky, and stars. These ziggurats were surrounded by temple complexes, open courtyards, and residences for the priests and priestesses.

Uruk became the base for the Sumerian civilization, which eventually dominated other areas of Mesopotamia. The rulers of the Sumerian civilization were kings who ruled by divine right, claiming the gods had given them the right to rule over people. One of the most famous kings, Gilgamesh, ruled around 4,500 years ago and built the famous walls of the city. His accomplishments were chronicled in the Epic of Gilgamesh, which is a poem that recounts Gilgamesh's adventures with monsters, gods, and goddesses (Mitchell, 2004). The epic of Gilgamesh was originally recorded in cuneiform, one of the earliest writing systems in the world.

Cuneiform evolved from pictograms, or pictures representing certain ideas, events, or people (Chazan, 2011). Over time, writing changed to signs of a more standardized script. Mesopotamian writing recorded daily events, trade, astronomy, and literature on clay tablets using cuneiform. A stylus, made from reed or wood, resembles a modern pencil with a wedge shape on one end, and was the main tool for writing cuneiform. This stylus is unique to the Mesopotamian writing system. The wedge was pressed into a clay or wax surface that could be "erased" and reused (Figure 7-2). Sometimes the clay or wax was spread onto boards made out of wood or ivory and could be easily transported. In other cases, the clay was a tablet that could be sent from one person to another for correspondence or keeping track of trade items.

Ur, a Sumerian city-state that flourished around 4,000 years ago, was located near the Euphrates River, but is currently several miles away from the Euphrates River, due to changes in the flow of the river over time. Ur was first excavated in the early 20th century and some of the major finds included the "royal tombs" and the Ziggurat of Ur (Woolley, 1927). The cemetery of Ur contained over 1,800 graves and sixteen of these graves were designated as "royal tombs." These tombs contained human sacrifices, had elaborate tomb construction, and included valuable objects that were imported from outside of Mesopotamia. One of these tombs, the tomb of Queen Puabi, had 52 individuals interred in a chamber near her burial tomb. In addition to these individuals, a wooden cart with two oxen skeletons was excavated, along with a wooden chest and a lyre (harp). Queen Puabi was buried with an elaborate gold headdress (Figure 7-3), a gold and lapis lazuli sculpture of a sheep or goat braced against a tree, and thousands of pieces of jewelry (Woolley, 1927). Another elaborate tomb contained 74 attendants (6 men and 68 women), all carefully laid out in the tomb. Similar to Queen Puabi's tomb, oxen were buried with a cart and attendants. In addition, a bull lyre made of wood, gold, and lapis lazuli was recovered from the main chamber of the tomb.

The Ziggurat of Ur was a monument composed of stepped towers made from mud brick and constructed around 4,000 years ago. King Ur-Nammu built the ziggurat to honor the moon god Nammu

Figure 7-4. Ziggurat of Ur (Image by Hardnfast).

and as part of a larger temple complex. The maximum dimensions of the Ziggurat are estimated as 210 feet long, 150 feet wide, and 100 feet tall. The temple complex probably included places for religious rituals, but may also have been used for governmental meetings. For example, King Ur-Nammu could have met visiting dignitaries at this impressive structure. Most of the site was excavated in the mid-19th century and a partial reconstruction was conducted in the 1980s by the Iraqi government (Figure 7-4).

7.2 AKKADIA

The Akkadian Empire was founded by King Sargon around 4,300 years ago in Mesopotamia. After taking power in the city of Kish, Sargon moved on to conquer other Mesopotamian cities, such as Uruk, Nippur, Eridu, and Laggash. He established a capital city, known as Akkad. The city of Akkad is mentioned in texts, but has not yet been discovered in modern times. King Sargon, also referred to in texts as "Sargon the Great," not only conquered Sumeria, but also expanded his empire into other territories to the northwest and southeast (Figure 7-5). By doing so, he gained control of silver and lapis lazuli mines, timber, and other important natural resources.

The economy of the Akkadian Empire was built on expansion, agriculture, and trade. Grain and other goods were distributed in standardized vessels made by potters who worked in artisan areas of the Akkadian cities (Fagan, 2004). Taxes were paid in grain, wool, meat, milk, cheese, and/or labor on public structures, such as walls, temples, and irrigation canals. The cities within the empire were connected by well-constructed roads and a postal system. During Sargon's reign, while there was constant warfare to expand the empire, there was also prosperity from the trade.

Figure 7-5. Bronze head attributed to Sargon, but it could also be his grandson, Naram-Sin.

Figure 7-6. Code of Hammurabi, the code is written in cuneiform and King Hammurabi is seated at the top.

After Sargon's death, his sons and grandsons maintained the Akkadian Empire until 4,100 years ago, approximately 180 years after Sargon's campaign to control Mesopotamia began. His sons and grandsons ruled despite several rebellions. In addition, several of his daughters and granddaughters became powerful priestesses. Around 4,100 years ago, however, drought and rebellion brought an end to the Akkadian Empire and a brief Sumerian renaissance arose. However, the Akkadian Empire's innovations in technology, infrastructure, and government continued to influence Mesopotamia.

7.3 BABYLONIA

Babylonia was an ancient culture in southern Mesopotamia and its capital city was Babylon. Babylonia became a major power when King Hammurabi, the sixth king of Babylon, consolidated his power (Leick, 2003). He began to expand the empire, conquering the city-states of Isin, Eshnunna, Uruk, and Mari; the Babylonia Empire eventually encompassed the territories of the Akkadian Empire. However, the earlier Akkadian and Sumerian traditions played a major role in Babylonian culture, and trade and agriculture continued to be the main forces in the economy.

King Hammurabi is most famous for compiling a law code that would standardize contracts, wages, divorce, judicial decisions, and military service. The law code, known as the "Hammurabi Code," standardized a wide variety of economic and societal issues (Scarre, 2005). It also normalized punishments for violations of the codes. Approximately half of the code deals with employment contracts, such as wages and extent of work. Other contractual issues relate to property damage and liability. About one-third of the code focuses on household and family issues such as inheritance, divorce, and paternity. The remaining sections of the code relate to judicial decisions and military service. One of the most famous parts of the codes is the adjusting of reimbursement for theft or other crimes in a like manner, thus perhaps being the origin of the biblical term, "an eye for an eye" (Driver and Miles, 2007). The code is also scaled for a person's social status or whether they are a slave or free. There are many copies of the Hammurabi code, written in cuneiform in the Akkadian language. However, the most famous is an almost complete copy, carved on diorite (Figure 7-6). It is a large upright stone, known as a stele, wider at the bottom, tapering at the top, and over seven feet high.

The Babylonian Dynasty came to an end around 2,500 years ago when King Cyrus, from lands to the west of Mesopotamia (what is Iran today), invaded. The last King of Babylon, Nabonidus, is documented as being a good military leader, but not very popular with the people he governed. One of his offenses was that he had elevated the Moon god Sin to prevalence in the Babylonian Empire, which offended the followers of the god Marduk (god of water, vegetation, and judgment). King Cyrus believed he was saving the people when he invaded and ousted King Nabonidus.

7.4 ASSYRIA

The Assyrian Empire originated in northern Iraq on the western bank of the Tigris River (Healy, 1991). Beginning around 4,500 years ago, the capital city of Assur was built up with multiple structures layered on top of each other. This type of construction eventually leads to an archaeological phenomenon known as a tell. A tell is a heap of compacted bricks, pottery, and stones formed by remains from ancient settlements. This occurs often in areas where water is localized, such as the Middle East, so people stay and rebuild in one place (Figure 7-7). Excavated in the late 19th and early 20th centuries, the site contained hundreds of houses, public structures, and cuneiform tablets.

Figure 7-7. A Middle Eastern Tell (Image by Gugganji).

Other cities in the Assyrian Empire contained some of the most elaborate palaces constructed in Mesopotamia. These palaces demonstrated the wealth and achievements of the Assyrian Empire. Around 2,800 years ago, King Ashurnasirpal II of Assyria made Nimrud his capital and built an elaborate palace near the Tigris River. Excavated in the mid-19th and 20th centuries, the palace was constructed from mud-brick and baked-brick walls. Excavations uncovered sculptures carved in bas-relief on the palace walls or made from ivory, stone, and clay. Some of the most dramatic statues are the large, winged lions with human heads that are estimated to weigh over 20,000 pounds and are over 15 feet tall (Figure 7-8). The statues are currently housed at the British Museum.

Bas-relief sculptures of Ashurnasirpal II decorated the walls of the palace at Nimrud. Most of the sculptures depict warfare, with images of men preparing for battle, the battles themselves, and Ashurnasirpal II accepting the defeat of his enemies. Sculptures of hunts depict the king in a chariot drawing his bow before killing a lion. He is surrounded by bodyguards holding shields and spears and a servant with an umbrella to shade him. Obviously, it is a symbolic representation of his might in battle, showing his willingness to raise arms (draw his bow) and hunt powerful opponents (Figure 7-9). King Ashurnasirpal II established a powerful dynasty that lasted for many centuries.

The palace at Nimrud was a huge complex that contained storage areas, rooms for scribes, royal receiving rooms, and private royal chambers. In addition, underneath the palace at Nimrud are the royal tombs. They were first discovered during excavations in the late 19th century. The tombs are all of queens and date to around 2,700 years ago. One tomb is that of Queen Yaba, who was the wife of Tiglathpileser III, another is Queen Banitu, wife of Shalmanasser V, and the last is Queen Atalia, wife of Sargon II. Buried in stone or bronze sarcophagi, the queens' tombs included thousands of pieces of elaborate jewelry made from gold, silver, bronze, precious stones, and lapis lazuli. The treasures in these royal tombs rival

Figure 7-8. Winged Colossal Statues from Nimrud (Image by Mujtaba Chohan).

those found in the more famous Royal Tombs of Ur. Eventually, though, the power and influence of the Assyrians came to an end 2,600 years ago after the death of King Ashurbanipal, which led to a series of civil wars and, ultimately, the conquering of Assyria by the Persian Empire.

7.5 BRINGING IT TOGETHER

Figure 7-9. Close-up of Sculpture from Nimrud depicting Ashurnasirpal II hunting lions (Image by Ealdgyth).

In this chapter, we learned about the development of a region known as Mesopotamia. This region encompassed what is modern-day Iraq and was largely concentrated in the Tigris and Euphrates river valleys. Beginning around 6,000 years ago, we see widespread agriculture and the development of some of the earliest cities in the world. One of the earliest cities is the city of Uruk, which contained many dwellings made of mud-brick. Also, public structures, known as ziggurats, were constructed for worshipping the gods. Later, the great city of Ur evolved, also with a ziggurat and multiple royal tombs containing a rich array of artifacts and humans sacrificed to be buried with the kings and queens. The Akkadian Empire follows with the powerful King Sargon taking over the city of Kish and moving on to conquer other Mesopotamian cities, such as Uruk and Ur. The Akkadian Empire lasted for about 180 years and covered vast territory, which was managed through a well-maintained road system and efficient postal system. Eventually, Babylon became the center of power in Mesopotamia and by the time of the sixth ruler, King Hammurabi, the Babylonia Empire encompassed much of the Tigris-Euphrates River Valley. King Hammurabi developed a code of laws, known as the Hammurabi Code, which established guidelines for employment, family disputes, punishments, and military service. The Assyrian Empire originated in northern Iraq around 4,500 years ago and eventually spread through Mesopotamia. Powerful kings, such as Ashurnasirpal II, pushed the boundaries of the empire to the northwest and southeast and built beautiful palaces at the capital city of Nimrud. Eventually, the dominance of the Mesopotamian empires waned as the power of the Persian Empire to the west increased.

Key Terms and Concepts

Mesopotamia	Comes from Greek and means "between the rivers," located in the Tigris and Euphrates river valleys that flow through modern Iraq, Syria, and Turkey.
Uruk	One of the earliest cities in the world, located along the Euphrates River, and established around 6,000 years ago.
Sumeria	A civilization, which eventually dominated lower Mesopotamia. Sumeria also refers to an ancient, non-semitic language family spoken by people from southern Iraq.

Ziggurat	A large structure, made of mud brick and stone, that was used for religious rituals.
Gilgamesh	Ruled Uruk around 4,500 years ago and built the famous walls of the city. Featured in the "Epic of Gilgamesh."
Cuneiform	The earliest form of writing in the world and was created by using a series of symbols impressed in clay or wax that represent certain ideas, events, or people.
Ur	A city near the Euphrates River that flourished around 4,000 years ago; contains the Ziggurat of Ur and the Royal Tombs of Ur.
Babylonia	An ancient cultural region in southern Mesopotamia and its capital city was Babylon.
King Hammurabi	Babylonian king who is most famous for compiling a law code
Hammurabi Code	Law code that standardized contracts, wages, divorce, judicial decisions, and military service.
Assyria	An empire originating in northern Iraq on the western bank of the Tigris River, eventually spread through much of Mesopotamia.
Tell	A heap of compacted bricks, pottery, and stones formed by remains from ancient settlements.
Assur	Capital city of Assyria.
King Ashurnasirpal II	Ruled Assyria and built the city of Nimrud. A powerful king who expanded the Assyrian Empire.
Palace of Nimrud	Elaborate palace built by King Ashurnasirpal II. It was constructed from mud-brick and baked-brick walls, and contained numerous sculptures and the tombs of three queens.

8: NORTH AFRICA

8.1 PREDYNASTIC EGYPT

The basic element in the lengthy history of Egypt is location, location, location. The Nile River, at the heart of Egypt, rises from the lakes of central Africa as the White Nile and from the mountains of Ethiopia as the Blue Nile. The White Nile and Blue Nile meet at Khartoum and flow together northward to the Nile delta, where the 4,000-mile river ends at the Mediterranean Sea. The source of the Nile is known as Upper Egypt and where the Nile disgorges into the Mediterranean is known as Lower Egypt. The cycle of flooding, caused by seasonal rains near the source of the Nile, is what makes the river valley so fertile for crops. Thus, the Egyptian civilization developed in a river valley, which is similar to the Mesopotamian civilizations we discussed in Chapter 7.

Around 7,000 years ago we begin to see farming, with plants like oil palm, yams, cowpea, pearl millet, sorghum, barley, and emmer wheat cultivated. Domestic animals included cattle, sheep, goats, donkeys, pigs, and dogs, but cattle were particularly important for plowing, as well as providing milk, butter, hides, and meat (Blench and McDonald, 2000). By 5,500 years ago, large independent cities and villages were located in the valley. These cities began to consolidate power and became independent city-states, also known as proto-kingdoms, in the Nile River Valley.

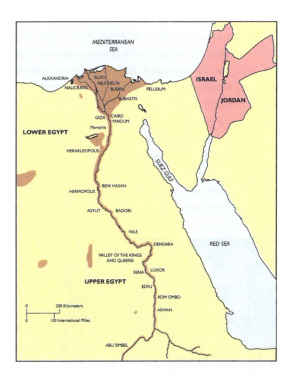

Figure 8-1.

There were four prominent proto-kingdoms in Egypt around 5,000 years ago, including Naqada, Hierakonpolis, Maadi, and Badari. Naqada was a walled city with cemeteries that was first excavated in the late 19th century.

Artifacts recovered from the site reveal that the people of Naqada traded for obsidian, cedar, and other materials. In the late 19th century, a prominent archaeologist named Sir Flinders Petrie unearthed three cemeteries at Naqada that contained 2,200 graves, the largest mortuary in pre-dynastic Egypt. Along with the human remains, Petrie found mud bricks, dog bones, and pottery. Other burial items included copper, ivory, bone, and shell jewelry; figurines of humans, oxen, and boats; and weapons and food.

Hierakonpolis (also known as Nekhen) was a major center that contained houses, cemeteries, temples, and administrative buildings (Wenke, 1991). The site also contains the oldest known tomb with painted walls and had the oldest zoo (World's First Zoo, 2012). Rulers of Hierakonpolis gained control of the surrounding area and formed political and social units. There was also an intensification of agriculture to feed an increasing population. Burial practices also became more intense and Hierakonpolis is a site were artificial mummification may have started. Over 200 burials have been excavated and one burial in particular, Burial 71, contains the remains of a 20- to 25-year-old woman whose head and hands were wrapped with linen and her internal organs were removed and wrapped in resin.

Maadi is located on the outskirts of modern Cairo and covered over 45 acres. It was a major trading center, as it was located on a former route to the copper mines of the Sinai Peninsula (Seeher, 1999). Copper was processed into tools, such as adzes. Adzes are axe-like implements used in woodworking, primarily for removing bark and shaping wood. There is also evidence of permanent houses and pottery, domesticated donkeys, storage facilities, and an advanced copper industry. Almost all of the houses were oval in shape and constructed with walls of wooden posts sealed with mud-daub. Pottery from Maadi was functional and plain, compared to the pottery found in dynastic Egypt. The deceased were buried in cemeteries, but were typically not buried with a lot of grave goods.

Finally, the settlement of Badari is also one of the earliest sites with evidence of agriculture during the Predynastic period (Wenke, 1991). The Badarian economy was mostly based on agriculture, fishing, and animal husbandry. Tools included axes, sickles, and arrowheads. The remains of cattle, dogs, and sheep were also found in the settlement and wheat, barley, lentils, and yams were grown. Outside of the main city, other, smaller settlements abounded. Mixed with these settlements were multiple cemeteries. Some cemeteries contained individuals with abundant grave goods and others had graves with little material, suggesting the there was clear social stratification in the region. This increasing social stratification and conflicts over control of the territories eventually gave rise to the dynastic periods, where all of Egypt was governed by one ruler.

Luckily, chronicles of early Egyptian life and the transition to an empire ruled by Pharaohs were recorded in the second-oldest writing system in the world. This form of writing, known as hieroglyphics, was written on papyrus scrolls, clay tablets, buildings, and monuments. Hieroglyphic writing combines symbols that represent something similar to the English alphabet, symbols representing ideas, and symbols that clarify those ideas. Most Egyptian writings chronicle the exploits of the Pharaohs, religious events and ceremonies, and everyday transactions, such as trade.

Egyptian writing was not completely deciphered until 1799 when Napoleon's troops found the Rosetta Stone (Figure 8-2), which was a royal decree recorded on a stone stele (Andrews, 1991). A stele is a stone monument that has images or writing to record important events. The decree was written in hieroglyphics,

Figure 8-2. The Rosetta Stone (Image by Hans Hellewaert).

Demotic (a later hieroglyphic script), and Greek. The stele was written 2,100 years ago and records that the Pharaoh Ptolemy V gave money to the temples and dammed the flooding waters of the Nile. Due to his largess, the decree stated that the priests would celebrate the birthday of Ptolemy V every year. The Greek writing on the stele provided the key for deciphering other hieroglyphic inscriptions.

While most official decrees were recorded on stone steles or monuments, the writing medium most common to the ancient Egyptians was papyrus scrolls. Papyrus was used to record trade, tribute and taxes paid to the Pharaohs, and official letters and notices. There were three kinds of writing used: hieroglyphic, hieratic, and demotic. Hieroglyphic was used primarily for monuments, tombs, and official documents. Hieratic was a form of hieroglyphic that was more cursive and had simplified symbols; this form was used for more casual writing, such as personal letters. Demotic was even more simplified and often one demotic symbol stood for many hieroglyphic symbols.

Figure 8-3. The Narmer Tablet.

8.2 EGYPTIAN DYNASTIES

The earliest record of dynastic Egypt is the Narmer tablet (Figure 8-3). King Narmer unified the city-states of Upper Egypt and Lower Egypt and established a capital at Thebes around 5,000 years ago (Chazan, 2011). He claimed that his unification of the city-states was divine intervention and that he ruled from the direct decree of the gods. Thus, he stood above the priests and was the only individual who had direct contact with the gods. Serving under the king were the priests and then other officials, the range of whom would be similar to governors or mayors who were in control of regions and cities in the Egyptian Empire. The rest of the population, including farmers, merchants, artists, and slaves, paid tribute or taxes to the pharaoh and were subject to laws and punishment established by the empire.

The unification of Egypt begins the dynastic period and starts with the Old Kingdom, goes through the Middle Kingdom, and ends with the New Kingdom. Interspersed between the kingdoms are "Intermediate Periods," which were periods when outsiders or the priests controlled Egypt. We will focus primarily on the kingdoms, but it is important to understand that the pharaohs were not always in control of their kingdoms. Some pharaohs were very young when they reigned and their regents made the decisions. Others were weak and either the priesthood or the advisors were influential or the empire was vulnerable to outside forces. The Old Kingdom reached its highest stage of development in the Fourth Dynasty. The most obvious markers of this period are the three pyramids built at Giza to house the remains of three pharaohs (Lehner, 1997), which were built between 4,600 and 4,500 years ago. The largest, built for the Pharoah Khufu, was originally almost 500 feet tall (Figure 8-4). Khufu's pyramid was constructed from stone blocks averaging over two tons each. There have been a lot of theories as to how long it took to build the pyramids, but some estimates suggest that it took over 100,000 workers twenty years to build (Kreis, 2002). Also, many people have marveled at how the pyramids were constructed.

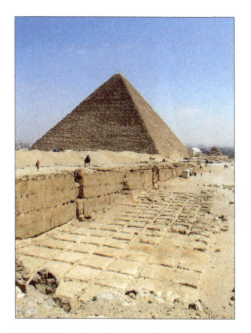

Figure 8-4. The Great Pyramid, built for the Pharaoh Khufu.

It is likely that the large blocks were carved from quarries, some located across the river from Giza and some that were over 500 miles away. They may have been dragged on wooden sleds or rolled on wooden rollers. Assembly at the site required some sort of scaffolding, or possibly a ramp, that allowed the workers to move the stones into place.

While many accounts suggest that the pyramids were built by slaves, more recent work suggests that there were certainly freemen, masons, and other specialists involved in the projects (Lehner, 1997; Verner, 2001). The pyramids are also part of a huge burial complex at Giza, which includes cemeteries, mastabas (one-story stone structures), queens' tombs, funerary temples, and the Great Sphinx. Finally, even though the pyramids were obvious symbols of the power of the pharaohs, unfortunately, all of them were looted in antiquity. Thus, in the Middle Kingdom and New Kingdom, pyramids for royal tombs were abandoned and other forms of burial monuments were sought, such as in the Valley of the Kings and Queens.

The first intermediate period began when the pharaoh's power diminished and the regional governors gained more autonomy over their provinces. These leaders proceeded to declare independence from the pharaohs and dynastic rule and began to increase their territories. The Middle Kingdom began when Menhutep II restored power around 4,000 years ago (Callender, 2000). He took power from the governors, by force if necessary, and re-established dynastic rule. Menhutep II ruled for 51 years and left a strong legacy when his son took power, as well as a large mortuary temple outside of Thebes.

The second Intermediate period began with an invasion by the Hyskos around 3,700 years ago. The Hyksos who came from the east systematically conquered the Nile River Valley. However, a Thebian Dynasty, led by Ahmose I, drove out the Hyksos and reunited the kingdom. Due to the domination of outsiders during the Second Intermediate Period, the pharaohs of the Eighteenth Dynasty created a government with a strong army to maintain control of the Nile Valley.

The Eighteenth Dynasty shepherded in the New Kingdom. One of the most powerful rulers of the New Kingdom was Ramesses II (also known as Ramses II). He ruled for 66 years after coming to power in his teens (Tyldesley, 2000). His early years as a ruler were spent organizing campaigns to extend the lands controlled by the empire, particularly in what is today Syria. He built many important public structures, such as his mortuary temple (the Ramesseum in Thebes), the religious temples of Abu Simbel, a new capital called Pi-Ramesses, and a large tomb in the Valley of the Queens for his Queen Nefertari. Nefertari was the favorite queen of Ramses II and her tomb contains many beautiful images of the queen and the king showing their piety to the gods to ensure the queen's passage into the afterlife. Ramesses II ruled for the longest period of any other Egyptian pharaoh and his construction projects outshone any other dynasty.

A powerful god in the Egyptian pantheon was the god Amun. Initially, Amun was a god who was the patron god of Thebes, but in the New Kingdom he became a nationally significant deity. His name was combined with the sun god Ra and he began to be referred to as Amun-Ra. Due to the power of the god, the priests who were responsible for the worship of Amun-Ra were very influential and controlled many of the pharaohs of the New Kingdom until Amenhotep IV came to the throne 3,300 years ago. He was determined to resist the power of the Amun-Ra priesthood and broke with the tradition of Amun-Ra such as significant deity. To do this, he moved his capital from Thebes (the center of Amun worship) to a city three hundred miles north (what is today El Amarna). This city's patron god was the god Aten, and he is depicted with a yellow disc representing the sun. Amenhotep IV changed his name to Akhenaten, which means "it pleases Aten," thus denying power to the Amun priesthood. This was the closest that Egypt really came to having a monotheistic religion.

After the death of Akhenaten, his chosen successor was put aside and replaced by Tutankaten, the son of Akhenaten and his wife, Nefertiti. The new pharaoh was very young when he took power—age eight or nine—and was apparently vulnerable to the Amun priesthood, because he restored the old religion and wiped many references to the worship of Aten in temples and palaces. He changed his name to Tutankamun and moved the capital back to Thebes.

Tutankamun was a minor king and lived too short a life (probably dying around the age of 19) to have any real accomplishments to his name. However, due to the nature of the archaeological record, it was his tomb that was discovered and his name is better known than some of the greater pharaohs, such as Khufu or Ramesses II. On November 26, 1922, Howard Carter found Tutankamun's tomb in the Valley of the Kings. Contrary to popular thinking, his tomb was robbed in antiquity, but the robberies probably occurred soon after his burial and the perpetrators caught and the materials returned to the tomb before it was resealed. His tomb contained many valuable artifacts, such as jewelry, thrones, chests, statues of gods, animal mummies, and of course, the sarcophagus and gold funerary mask of the pharaoh (Figure 8-5). The tomb also included two mummies of stillborn children; DNA tests have indicated they are the children of Tutankamun. Tutankamun's cause of death has long been speculated upon, but recent DNA tests and CAT scans indicate that he had weak bones (with a recently broken leg at the time of his death) and malaria. The leg break may have become infected and caused his death, according to Zahi Hawass, an Egyptologist and former Minister of State of Antiquities Affairs (Roberts, 2010).

Figure 8-5. The gold and lapis lazuli funerary mask of Pharaoh Tutankamun.

The completeness of Tutankamun's tomb allowed researchers to fully understand the mummification process. The Egyptians believed that an intact vessel (the mummy) was needed to complete the passage into the afterlife. The embalming process was a religious ritual and usually took around seventy days to complete in the case of the royals, but would take shorter amounts of time, depending on what the non-royal families could afford (Taylor, 2001). The internal organs (except for the heart) were removed and placed in ceremonial jars, known as canopic jars. These canopic jars had the heads of the main Egyptian deities. The brain was removed by hooking the brain through the nose, though in some cases the back of the skull may have been broken to remove the brain. The body was then packed with natron salt to dehydrate the remains. Finally, the body was coated with resin (sap) from trees and wrapped in resin-soaked cloths. This bundle was then placed into a sarcophagus, which in the case of the pharaohs, their queens and children were carved from wood and painted with the individual's face and religious symbols. We know from Tutankamun's mummy that the royal mummies also had an elaborate face mask with gold pectorals and religious symbols placed on the chest. The sarcophagus was then placed in a stone container for better preservation.

The Egyptian Dynasty continued until around 2,000 years ago, when the Ptolemaic Dynasty came to an end. The Ptolemys were a royal family of Macedonian Greek origins who took power in northern Egypt 2,300 years ago. The last pharaoh of this dynasty was Cleopatra VII, whose fascinating life has been chronicled in books and movies. Her famous love affairs with Caesar and Antony rocked two empires. Unfortunately, the story ended in tragedy when Cleopatra lost the empire, and subsequently her life through suicide, to the Roman Empire in 30 B.C. (Schiff, 2011).

8.3. BRINGING IT TOGETHER

The Egyptian civilization began around 5,000 years ago when King Narmer unified the Egyptian city-states and established the Egyptian dynastic period. Egyptian civilization went through several changes and is divided into periods called the Old Kingdom, Middle Kingdom, and New Kingdom. Interspersed between these kingdoms were periods of non-dynastic rule when either local governors, priests, or outside groups controlled the empire. The ancient Egyptians were famous for the massive public works, including pyramids, mortuary temples, and cities. The famous Egyptian pyramids were the tombs of some of the pharaohs of the Old Kingdom. The Valley of the Kings and Queens became the resting place of the royals during the New Kingdom. We know much of the Egyptian way of life due to hieroglyphic writing on many papyrus scrolls, temples, and monuments. The Rosetta Stone, discovered by Napoleon's troops, was the key to deciphering hieroglyphics. One of the most powerful pharaohs was Ramesses II who ruled for 66 years and constructed many important monuments. Pharaoh Tutankamun, while having only a lesser impact on the civilization at the time of his death, became famous for his intact tomb discovered by Howard Carter in 1922. The end of the Egyptian Empire occurred at the hands of the Romans, but the legacy of the dynastic period endures with the thousands of monuments, tombs, and temples in Egypt today.

Key Terms and Concepts

Nile River	Originally two rivers, the blue and the white, the Nile River flows north to the Mediterranean Sea.
Naqada	A pre-dynastic city state containing the largest mortuary complex in pre-dynastic Egypt.
Hierakonpolis	A major city-state that contained houses, cemeteries, temples, administrative buildings, the oldest known tomb with painted walls, and the oldest zoo.
Maadi	A city-state, located on the outskirts of modern Cairo, it was a major trading center on a route to the copper mines of the Sinai Peninsula.
Badari	A city-state with the earliest evidence of agriculture in the Pre-dynastic period, also had a large cemetery complex.

Hieroglyphics	One of the oldest writing systems in the world and combines symbols from an alphabet, symbols representing ideas, and symbols that clarify those ideas. Hieratic and Demotic are other, less formal, forms.
Rosetta Stone	A stone found by Napoleon's troops that has a royal decree written in Hieroglyphics, Demotic, and Greek. Was the key to deciphering hieroglyphics.
King Narmer	Unified upper and lower Egypt; his accomplishments are recorded on the Narmer tablet.
Old Kingdom	The first period of Dynastic Egypt.
First Intermediate Kingdom	A period when the pharaohs lost power and the provincial governors ruled.
Middle Kingdom	Menhutep II restored pharaonic rule.
Second Intermediate Kingdom	A period when outsiders, the Hyskos, controlled much of Egypt.
New Kingdom	Power restored to the pharaohs by Ahmose I.
Ramesses II	Probably the most powerful ruler in Egypt, he ruled for 66 years and built numerous monuments, temples, and statues.
Akhenaten	Born Amenhotep IV, he resisted the Amun priesthood, moved the capital to another city, and came close to monotheism with his worship of Aten.
Tutankamun	Born Tutankaten, the son of Akhenaten, came to power around the age of 9 and was largely controlled by the Amun priesthood, so he was renamed and the capital was moved back to Thebes.
Mummification	A process for preserving the dead that involved removing internal organs (except for the heart) and the brain, dehydrating the body with natron salt, and preserving the remains with resin-soaked cloths.
Cleopatra VII	The last Egyptian pharaoh, even though her dynasty was actually Macedonian Greek.

9: THE MEDITERRANEAN

9.1 MINOAN

The Mediterranean is an area of interesting cultural development that was heavily influenced by trade. The island of Crete, in the Mediterranean sea, was originally settled by Neolithic farmers around 9,000 years ago who came from the east (Broodbank and Strasser, 1991). They grew wheat, barley, grapes, figs, and olives, and herded sheep and goats. Also, most settlements along the coast fished and collected shellfish, squid, and octopus. Eventually, some of these settlements increased in size and also increased their influence through trade. The Minoans produced a civilization oriented around trade and bureaucracy with little or no evidence of a military state. Crete became the central exporter of wine, oil, and jewelry. They also traded tin, which was an important commodity in the Bronze Age for the making of bronze tools, weapons, and other items. To accomplish this expansion in trade, they eventually developed a major fleet of ships.

As we have discussed in earlier chapters, the onset of agriculture and increasing social complexity resulted in cities and civilizations. In the Minoan world, as the control over trade and shipping increased, there developed social stratification and some settlements became large enough to support kingdoms. In several places around the island, palaces were built and kings controlled territories around these palaces.

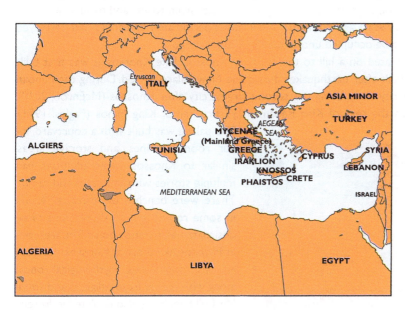

Figure 9-1.

Figure 9-2. Frescos in a room at Knossos (Image by Chris 73 Wikimedia Commons).

The Minoan chronology can be divided into the Pre-Palace, Old Palace, and the New Palace periods, based on construction and reconstruction of palace centers over time.

The Pre-Palace period begins with the intensification of settlement on Crete around 5,000 years ago. This is the time when the agriculture and trade mentioned previously proliferates. The Old Palace period began around 4,200 years ago and the oldest palaces on the island are Knossos and Phaistos. The site of Knossos is located just outside of the modern capital of Crete: Heraklion. It was excavated in the early 20th century by Arthur Evans, who also did some of the early reconstruction at the site (Castleden, 1990). Arthur Evans was interested in the site due to its fame in Greek mythology as the palace of King Minos and the famous labyrinth. Castleden argues that the early assumptions about the construction at Knossos as a palace are incorrect and that they are more accurately described as governing centers that included storehouses, meeting areas, a theater, and places of religious worship, as well as places where the kings and queens ruled. The structure at Knossos is laid out with buildings arranged around a central court area. Most of the external facades and interiors were constructed of stone blocks that were covered over with brightly painted frescoes, which are wall murals (Figure 9-2). The magazines were areas used for storage, and thousands of pithoi (large ceramic vases) were found filled with wine, olive oil, and other food remnants. In addition to the beautifully decorated rooms and storage areas, the Minoans and Knossos built a water system to supply water from springs near the site. They also had pipes and drainage systems for water runoff during the rainy season and a sewage system for draining waste water from toilets and baths (Castleden, 1990). Knossos was rebuilt around 3,700 years ago during the New Palace period after an earthquake destroyed much of the structure and continued to be occupied until around 3,100 years ago.

Phaistos is a Minoan palace site situated on a hill to the south of Knossos. Like Knossos, it was first built in the Old Palace period, and then rebuilt after earthquakes during the New Palace period. During the Minoan times, Phaistos was a very important city-state, being the second largest city after Knossos (McEnroe, 2010). According to mythology, Phaistos was the seat of King Radamanthys, brother of King Minos (Fagles, 1991).

Figure 9-3. Bull jumping fresco at Knossos.

The palace was built with a courtyard, inner rooms, shrines, and storage areas, similar to Knossos. Later additions had multiple stories with staircases and ramps. There were benches or "thrones" found in some rooms and so those were often designated as throne rooms. The frescoes at Phaistos, like those at Knossos, depicted animals (sometimes mythological ones) along with scenes from religious and social life. Bull jumping is also depicted in frescos (Figure 9-3). Apparently this was a sport for young men who would grab the horns

Figure 9-4. The Phaistos Disc (Image by Aserakov).

of running bulls and leap over their backs. Bulls' horns are also often depicted in Minoan palaces.

There are three types of pictographic writing that have been discovered in Minoan Crete. These are Linear A, Linear B, and the Phaistos Disc. Linear A is found in many places in Crete. Most examples are engraved on clay tablets, but there are some artifacts of metal with writing on them. Unfortunately, Linear A has not been translated. Like Egyptian writing before the recovery of the Rosetta Stone, there are no writings in Linear A that are repeated in a known script. Linear B has been found at only one site in Crete, at the palace at Knossos, but has been found in many places on mainland Greece and associated with the Mycenaen civilization. Linear B consists of both syllabic (a unit for a sound of speech) and ideographic (a symbol that represents an idea) and it is thought to be an early form of Greek. Only one example of the third type of writing has ever been found, and it is known as the Phaistos Disc (Belistier, 2000). It is on a decorative clay disc found at the palace at Phaistos and it dates to the first phase of the new palace period, around 3,700 years ago (Figure 9-4). The symbols are stamped in a spiral pattern on both sides of the disc. There is much debate as to whether the writing on the Phaistos disc represents an actual written language or if it depicts stylized images that are purely symbolic and not part of a writing system.

In Minoan religion, the main deity is female and referred to as a "Mother Goddess" (Marinatos, 1993). She is a symbol for fertility and protection and is often depicted in pottery and art holding snakes (Figure 9-5). Sacred objects depicting the goddess are found in palace temples, burials, and caves. Another image that is represented frequently in Minoan religion is the bull. The bull may have been the male aspect of fertility and life (Marinatos, 1993). Bulls' horns are found as decorations in many parts of the palace ruins and on ceramic vessels, seals, and ornaments. It has also been recorded that bulls were sacrificed in some religious ceremonies. The blood was collected and then poured onto columns in temples or in caves as a ritual offering. As mentioned above, ceremonies that involved leaping over bulls are represented in Minoan art and the ceremony may have been more ritual than sport.

Around 3,400 years ago, outside forces, particularly Mycenaen from mainland Greece, began to gain control of Crete. During this period people began to abandon settlements like Knossos and Phaistos that were near the coast and move to the mountains of the interior for better protection. An example of this is the Bronze Age village of Vronda, near Kavousi, Crete (Gesell et al., 1995). Vronda was abandoned in the late Bronze Age and people moved to the more defensible site of Kastro. The abandoned site of Vronda, however, continued to be used as a burial site and many "goddess vessels," pottery vases of goddesses holding snakes, were recovered.

Figure 9-5. Minoan Goddess Vessel (Image by Chris 73/Wikimedia Commons).

9.2 MYCENAEN

Beginning around 3,900 years ago, on the area of mainland Greece called the Peloponnese peninsula a civilization known as the Mycenaens developed. The Mycenaens developed their culture and controlled territory mainly through warfare. They also traded over great distances, generally trading grapes and grape products (oil and wine), olives, wheat, barley, wool, and perfume and copper and iron ore (Castledon, 2005). In addition to warfare and trade, the Mycenaens are known for their exceptional artwork and elaborate tombs. Pottery is represented in a variety of forms, including vases, pitchers, and cups. Also, statues of female figures and bull horns may represent religious items similar to those found in Minoan Crete. In addition, frescoes found in palaces and other buildings depict female figures, bulls, and warfare (Castledon, 2005). The dead were buried in cemeteries, with upper-class individuals interred in elaborate tombs containing artifacts made from gold, copper, bronze, and ceramics.

Figure 9-6. The Lions Gate at Mycenae (Image by David Monniaux).

By 3,600 years ago, the cities of the Mycenaen civilization were impressive semi-fortresses that were evidence of the power of the Mycenaen rulers. Initially, some of the cities were thought to be only legendary stories by Greek scholars. In stories by Homer, Mycenae is the capital city of King Agamemnon who laid siege to Troy over the famous Helen (Fagles, 1991). However, in the late 19th century, archaeologist Heinrich Schliemann found the city called Mycenae, located in the south central part of what is present-day Greece. During the Bronze Age, the city was a fortified, hilltop settlement surrounded by a large stone wall (Castledon, 2005). The main entrance was located in the western part of the city and the gate was topped by two lions, thus it is known as the Lions Gate (Figure 9-6). In addition to a central palace, there were houses, religious sanctuaries, markets, and storage areas located within the walls. Clay tablets of Linear B writing were discovered in the storage areas and were mostly lists of materials and goods and were probably used for record keeping. The city center is probably where the upper-class citizens lived, while farmers, slaves, and other lower-class citizens lived at the base of the hill. Cemeteries and tombs were located outside the city walls.

The Mycenaen civilization began to decline around 3,200 years ago, probably due to warfare between cities. It may be that the rulers of these cities had grown very powerful and were looking to expand their territories. Many of the cities show signs of more defensive structures, supporting this hypothesis. Eventually, the cities were abandoned and Mycenaen influence in the region ceased.

9.3 ETRUSCAN

The Etruscan civilization evolved in eastern Italy near the Tyrrhenian Sea around 2,700 years ago (Bonfonte, 1990). This civilization stretched from the Arno River to the Tiber River. Although located to the east of Crete and Greece, their inclusion in this chapter is due to their "Mediterranean-like lifestyle." For example, their agriculture was focused on growing grapes, olives, and wheat; their domestic animals included sheep, goats, and cattle, which is very similar to the Minoan and Mycenaen civilizations. The Etruscans lived in city-states that were fortified with walls and built on hilltops where possible. Initially, these city-states were independent and had their own rulers; later a government consisting of a small number of powerful rulers governed the region as a whole.

The Etruscans are well known from their elaborate tombs, which typically included more than one person and were used for multiple generations. One well-documented cemetery is in the town of Cerveteri and is the Necropolis of Banditaccia (Unesco World Heritage Centre, 2012). The necropolis is spread over one and a half miles and has over 1,000 graves that date between 2,800 and 2,200 years ago. Some of the mounds contain pits with cremated remains, but the more elaborate ones are large mounds with uncremated remains. The burial tombs at the necropolis are laid out in neat rows and have open areas; this layout was very deliberately planned and resembles a city center. The inner chambers of the mounds are made to resemble domestic houses and contain fresco-covered walls, sculptures, grave goods that usually reflect household activities, and inscriptions (Etruscan Necropolises, 2012). The best-known tomb at the site is called the Tomb of Reliefs and contains frescos that are particularly detailed. Finally, during the later stages of tomb construction, cylindrical stones were placed in front of tombs if they had males interred inside and stones shaped liked houses if women were interred. These stone markers are known as cippi.

Like the Mycenaens, the Etruscans also were strong militarily and expanded their territories through warfare. People conquered by the Etruscans often became laborers on farms and in mines to help increase production. This also allowed Etruscans to invest that surplus from increased production in trade. The scope of trade included trading wine, olive oil, wool, and bronze artifacts for materials like Greek pottery. Etruscan shipwrecks have been recovered from as far away as the coast of France.

Etruscans did have a writing system and it was mainly found on tombs and monuments. It is unfortunate that, although the words can be pronounced (due to a similarity with the Greek alphabet), no translations for the words have survived. There are over 10,000 Etruscan inscriptions, which are mainly in tombs or sanctuaries. Others engravings are found on bronze sculptures, coins, and ceramic vessels. Despite the lack of translated Etruscan writings, we know from Greek and Roman records that conflicts between Etruscans, Greeks, and Romans around 2,200 years ago resulted in the reduction of power for Etruscans. Eventually, the Romans in the south of Italy began to dominate the peninsula, Etruscan cities became Romanized, and the knowledge about Etruscan writing and culture disappeared.

9.4 BRINGING IT TOGETHER

We explored the Minoan, Mycenaen and Etruscan civilizations in this chapter. The Minoans evolved on the island of Crete and the civilization is best known for its large palaces at Knossos and Phaistos. These palaces contained areas where the Kings governed, which were usually elaborately decorated with frescoes. The palaces were also areas that redistributed resources, such as olive oil and grain, as evidenced by storage rooms. Evidence for writing at the palaces takes three forms, but it is only Linear B that has been translated due to its similarity to ancient Greek. The Mycenaen civilization was located on mainland Greece and essentially took power through military excursions throughout the mainland and islands. Mycenae, the capital city, was a walled fortress with a main entrance known as the Lions Gate. Cemeteries were located outside the city walls and elaborate tombs reflect the status typical of the ruling families of Mycenae. Finally, the Etruscan civilization, while something of an enigma to scholars, evolved around 2,700 years ago in what is today Italy. The Etruscans are known for their cemeteries laid out like cities and tombs with beautiful frescoes. The Etruscan language, while well represented in the archaeological record, has not been translated. Rome, located in the south of Italy, became the dominant power in the region around 2,200 years ago and eventually replaced Etruscan culture in the north.

Key Terms and Concepts

Minoan	Civilization on the island of Crete, beginning around 4,200 years ago.
Knossos	Palace of the Minoan civilization on the north side of the island containing government offices, royal chambers, religious sanctuaries, and storage areas. Elaborate frescos decorate the walls of the palace.
King Minos	King of Knossos, Crete.
Pithoi	Large ceramic vases used for storage.
Phaistos	Palace of the Minoan civilization on the south side of the island.
Linear A	Found in many places in Crete, most examples are engraved on clay tablets, has not been translated.
Linear B	Consists of both syllabic (a unit for a sound of speech) and ideographic (a symbol that represents and idea). It is thought to be an early form of Greek.
Phaistos disc	Disc with writing found at Phaistos that has not been translated.
King Radamanthy	King of Phaistos, Crete.
Minoan religion	Mother Goddess represented as well as bulls that may represent males.
Mycenaen	Civilization on mainland Greece that took over Minoan civilization around 3,900 years ago and dominated the region.
Mycenae	City of the Mycenaen civilization famous for its being the city of King Agamemnon from Homer's Iliad.
King Agamemnon	King of Mycenae, Greece.
Lions gate	Main entrance of the city of Mycenae.
Etruscan	Civilization in east-central Italy, beginning around 2,700 years ago, strong in trade and military.

Necropolis of Banditaccia Etruscan cemetery containing tombs decorated with frescos.

Cippi Stone markers in front of tombs with cylindrical markers indicating a male's tomb and dome-shaped markers (house shaped) indicating a female's tomb.

10: EAST ASIA

10.1 EARLY CULTURES IN JAPAN

East Asia has a diverse history with settlement of early hominins as early as 1,000,000 years ago. Early modern humans arrived in East Asia approximately 30,000–60,000 years ago and lived as hunters and gatherers. As the population increased, some groups became more sedentary and this marks the beginning of the Neolithic period. The Neolithic period in Japan is known as the Jōmon period and it is characterized by semi-sedentary hunter-gatherers who subsisted on freshwater fish, shellfish, deer, and wild plants (Habu, 2004). Even though they were hunters and gatherers, the earliest people in Japan had pottery for cooking and storing food, which is the earliest pottery in the world, dating to around 10,000 years ago (Figure 10-2). This is unusual because it is mostly agriculturalists who have pottery; they do not move around a lot and therefore do not risk breaking the fragile ceramics. The Jōmon villages had houses that were semi-subterranean and were likely constructed by

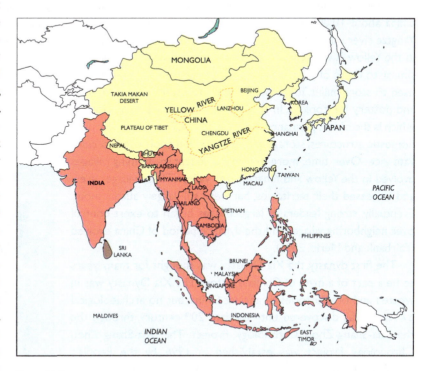

Figure 10-1.

digging a shallow oval or circular pit, then making walls of small tree limbs or trunks packed with mud, and covering the structure with a thatched roof. The early people of Japan continued to hunt, gather, and fish for their food until rice and millet agriculture was introduced around 3,000 years ago. Other Neolithic period Japanese cultures include the Yayoi and the Kofun. The Yayoi period is best known for the making of bronze and iron objects, in addition to practicing agriculture. The Kofun period marked a more militaristic period that transitioned into the Classical period with a centralized state.

Classical Japan is bracketed by the Asuka period, with a centralized state, a law system and the introduction of Buddhism and the Heian period, which was characterized as a highly imperialistic time in Japanese history (Hall, 1993). The Classical period lasted from between 1,500 years ago and ended around 900 years ago. The following period, known as the Medieval period was characterized by strong ruling families who controlled populations of peasants and workers and had strong militaries. The Medieval period ended around 400 years ago, when the Edo period began. During the Edo period, leaders (called shoguns) centralized religion, standardized the economy (which was mostly rice production), and made advances in writing, art and architecture (Hall, 1993). Modern and contemporary Japan followed this time and began in the mid 1800s.

10.2 EARLY CULTURES IN CHINA

The earliest period in China is known as the "Ancient" period and includes the Neolithic era, and the Xia, Shang, and Zhou dynasties. This period dates to between 12,000 and 2,200 years ago. The Neolithic period begins in China about 10,000 years ago. It is defined by a spread of settled agricultural communities in the Yellow and Yangtze river valleys (Fairbank and Merle, 2006). Millet, one of the earliest East Asian cultigens, was domesticated in the Yellow River Valley. The site of Cishan consisted of numerous pit houses (semi-subterranean structures, similar to those of the Jōmon period), the remains of pigs, dogs, and chickens, and hundreds of deep pit features used to store millet. Tools found that were used to cultivate millet included stone spades, mortars and pestles, and pottery for cooking. In the Yangtze River Valley, early rice cultivation is evidenced at the Pengtoushan site, which is the oldest permanent village in China. The Pengtoushan site, similar to the Cishan site, contained multiple domestic structures, storage pits, pottery, and tools used to cultivate rice. Over time, more and more sedentary farming villages evolved in the Yellow and Yangtze river valleys. These villages grew and increased their territories, but were still largely autonomous. Eventually, strong leaders of large villages began to exert control over neighboring villages and the dynastic period of China evolved (Fairbank and Merle, 2006).

The first dynasty, the Xia Dynasty, was thought for many years to be a part of a myth of Chinese history. The Xia Dynasty was in written and oral histories of ancient China, but no archaeological evidence was discovered until the late 20th century through the the Xia-Shang-Zhou Chronology Project. The Xia-Shang-Zhou Chronology Project was established in 1996 by the People's Republic of China to document these early dynasties (Li, 2002). Excavations at sites like Erlitou, believed to be the capital of the Xia Dynasty, indicate the Xia Dynasty started around 4,000 years ago.

Figure 10-2. Jōmon pottery vessel.

Erlitou, is located in the modern city of Yanshi, eventually grew to be an urban center with a population of around 20,000–30,000 people, palaces and temples, roads, and bronze workshops.

The Xia Dynasty eventually lost power, and the Shang Dynasty (originally centered in the Yellow River Valley) took over around 3,600 years ago. Archaeological work at Yinxu, the Shang capital, revealed eleven royal tombs containing thousands of bronze, jade, stone, bone, and ceramic artifacts. In addition, the remnants of palaces and temples were also discovered. One of the most important innovations of the Shang Dynasty is the development of a writing system. The Chinese writing system is logographic (a combination of pictographs, ideographs, aggregates, and phonetic characters). The most common place for the earliest writings are found on oracle bones and used for divination (Figure 10-3). The bones used for this purpose originally came from a number of animals, but were eventually done exclusively on turtle shells. A question was written on the bone, which was then heated until it began to crack. The locations of the cracks were used to interpret the answer to the question by a diviner. Then, after the event occurred (presumably as predicted), the events were described on the bone. Many oracle bone questions were written to the god Shangdi. This god was a supreme god and was thought to control human events, such as warfare, the weather, and politics.

Figure 10-3. Shang Dynasty oracle bone.

The final "Ancient" dynasty was the Zhou. The Zhou were largely nomadic until they settled in the Wei River Valley. They eventually became stronger than the Shang, and about 3,000 years ago they defeated the Shang and claimed their territories. Part of the Zhou's success was in gaining the allegiance of other city-states in the region. The Zhou capital was Xi'an, located on the Yellow River, and they controlled the capital and territories with a strict hierarchy of royals, with the king at the pinnacle. There was a clear division between the royal families and the merchants, farmers, and laborers in the dynasty. All lands were owned by the royal families, with a portion of the crops (or pottery or bronze) given each year to build the royal treasury.

The Zhou Dynasty is marked by warfare and expansionism, so the resources that went into the military were tremendous. However, they did make great advances in agriculture, developing extensive irrigation systems to increase production. There were also great accomplishments in religion and philosophy. They abandoned the Shang's worship of Shangdi in favor of a more universal concept of the heavens (Gernett, 1996). The famous philosophers, Confucius, who founded Confucianism, and Laozi, who founded Taoism, lived during this time (Dawson, 1982; Kirkland, 2004).

10.2 IMPERIAL CHINA

The Zhou Dynasty ended with the conquering of its territories by the Qin Dynasty. The Qin controlled so much territory in China that it was essentially an empire. Thus, the Qin Dynasty marks the beginning of the Imperial period 2,200 years ago. The leader who formed the empire named himself the First Emperor, or Shi Huang, thus beginning the tradition of having emperors for rulers. The Qin had a very strong military and they used

Figure 10-4. The tomb of Shi Huang featuring the Terra Cotta Army.

new technology, particularly equipment (such as crossbows) related to the development of a cavalry. The Qin are sometimes called the Ch'in, which is probably where the name China originated. Other than military accomplishments, the Qin also made several social changes. First, they standardized the language and writing of their territories. Also, currency became standardized. Currency was usually made out of bronze or copper, circular in shape, and with a square hole in the middle. Measurements and axle length were also made uniform. This was done because the cartwheels made ruts in the road, and the ruts had to all to be the same width, or carts with a different axle length could not travel on them. They also began building one of the Great Walls to protect the northern borders (Lewis, 2007). Most people think of just one Great Wall when they think of China, but there were actually multiple walls built throughout China for protection from the north.

The Qin Dynasty is also famous for the burial site of Shi Huang, known as the "Tomb of the Terra Cotta Soldiers". The tomb, which was originally a mound 140 feet high, was discovered in 1974 (Mausoleum, 2012). Excavations of the tomb revealed an army of thousands of soldiers, made from terra cotta, which may have been placed there to ceremonially protect the burial chamber of Shi Huang. There were also horses and chariots in some of the pits and weapons such as spears, bows and arrows, shields, and crossbows. Although the complete tomb has not been excavated, it is estimated that over 6,000 soldiers came from one of the pits (Figure 10-4). Each of the soldiers had a carefully crafted and painted uniform and their faces, beards, and hair are very individualized, suggesting that actual people or soldiers may have posed for the craftsmen working on the tomb (Figure 10-5). The actual burial chamber of Shi Huang has not been opened so the remains can be preserved in their original state. Shi Huang longed for a long life, so he sent his doctors, priests, and ministers to go on quests to find a potion for immortality. It is suspected that when he died it was due to consuming some of these potions that may have contained mercury (Wright, 2011).

After the death of Shi Huang, the Qin Dynasty was in turmoil and the Han Dynasty came to power. The Han Dynasty made particular improvements in the economy, particularly with trade. They expanded trade in areas to the west and this is essentially when the trade route known as the Silk Road developed. Parts of the Great Wall were also constructed to protect this trade route. During the Han Dynasty, there were also improvements in agriculture, such as iron plows and wheelbarrows (Needham, 1972). Another innovation was the development of paper. As discussed previously, early writing was done primarily on animal bones for divination. Later, engravings were made on bronze objects. Paper made from bamboo was also used and this was much more portable and could be used for official documents. Following the end of the Han Dynasty, there was a period of political unrest.

Figure 10-5. Closeup of the Terra Cotta Soldiers (Image by Tomasz Sienicki).

Eventually, the short-lived Sui Dynasty (who also expanded the Great Wall) and then the Tang Dynasty re-established dynastic rule (Gernet, 1996). The Tang Dynasty was known for its stability and social innovations. They established a census and around 1,400 years ago and the estimated population was 50 million (Ebrey, 1999). The census was used to establish a system of taxation for people. They also developed wood block printing and were able to mass produce books and other writings. One of these documents was the Tang Code. This is the first complete Chinese code that still exists and it consists of penalties that are given depending on the crime and the relationship between the suspect and the victim. The Tang Code had more than five hundred articles divided into twelve sections and the sections dealt with specific crimes, such as forgery, tax violations, desecration of sacred places, military and government violations, and family issues (Gernet, 1996).

Following the Tang Dynasty, there was a period of unrest until the Song Dynasty reestablished control over the empire. Accomplishments of the Song Dynasty are the establishing of a paper money system, the development of a navy, and the invention of gunpowder (Gernet, 1996). Despite these innovations, and ruling for over 300 years, the Song Dynasty fell to the "northern hordes," or the Mongols. The leader Kublai Khan succeeded where his predecessors had failed and became ruler of much of China (Ebrey, 1999). The Mongols ruled China for only a hundred years before the Ming regained control in the 14th century. The Ming reestablished the government and made great strides in the arts. The Ming Dynasty is particularly well known for its poetry, painting, music, and decorative arts. Decorative items such as porcelain vases, jade carvings, gold statues, and lacquer boxes are some of the most beautiful in the world (Figure 10-6). Finally, the last dynasty was the Qing Dynasty, which took power from the Ming in the 17th century and controlled China until the 20th century when dynastic power came to an end. The Qing Dynasty is best known as being one of the largest empires in the world at its height and controlled a territory that included China, Tibet, and Mongolia. Eventually, rebellions caused the end of dynastic China and China became the People's Republic of China.

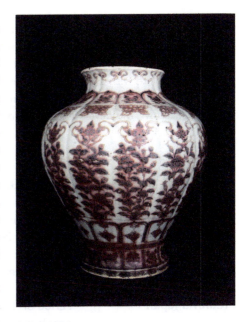

Figure 10-6. Ming vase.

10.3 BRINGING IT TOGETHER

The Ancient and Imperial periods of China saw the development of much of the Asian continent from a nomadic lifestyle with hunting and gathering societies, to agriculturalists, to one of the largest empires of the world. During the early Jōmon period in Japan, people settled in the area and lived as hunters and gatherers, and through fishing and collecting shellfish. On mainland China, people began to domesticate millet in the Yellow River Valley and rice in the Yangtze River Valley. Eventually, the increase in population led to the development of large settlements, such as Cishan and Pengtoushan. In time, leaders in these areas began to control broader territories and the early dynasties, such as the Xia, developed. The Xia Dynasty was located in northern China and its capital was Erlitou. Following the Xia Dynasty, the Shang Dynasty developed innovations in agriculture and invented the earliest writing system in China, which were Chinese characters written on oracle bones. Following the Shang, the Zhou Dynasty expanded control over China through warfare and controlled most of northern China. The Qin Empire ushered in the true imperial period in China and its powerful first Emperor, Shi Huang, built a huge tomb complex, complete with a terra cotta army to protect him in the afterlife. The imperial dynasties had amazing innovations, such as standardized money, standardized roads, a unified language and writing system, iron plows and wheelbarrows, the development of gunpowder, and a system of penalties for crimes committed against its citizens.

Key Terms and Concepts

Jōmon — Period characterized by semi-sedentary hunter-gatherers who subsisted on freshwater fish, shellfish, deer, and wild plants.

Classical Japan — Includes the Asuka and Heian periods.

Medieval Japan — Period of "feudalism" in Japan with most of the population farming rice and few people in power. Also, a time of great warfare.

Edo period — Period in Japan that standardized the government, religion and writing. Increase in art, culture, and architecture.

Neolithic period — Begins in China about 10,000 years ago. It is defined by a spread of settled agricultural communities in the Yellow and Yangtze river valleys.

Rice and millet — Early domestic plants cultivated in the Yellow and Yangtze river valleys.

Cishan and Pengtoushan — Early Neolithic sites in China.

Xia Dynasty — The first dynasty of China, previously thought to be a myth. The capital city is Erlitou.

Shang Dynasty — An ancient Chinese dynasty with the first writing system on oracle bones.

Oracle bones — Used for divination in ancient China by writing questions on the bones and heating them until they cracked, diviners could tell the future based on the patterns of cracks.

Zhou Dynasty — The last of the ancient Chinese dynasties.

Qin Dynasty — First imperial dynasty. Established a standard monetary system and standardized the width of roads. Shi Huang was the first emperor.

Shi Huang — First emperor, Qin Dynasty, built a huge tomb that was surrounded by a terra cotta army.

Han Dynasty	Follows the Qin dynasty, expanded trade through the Silk Road, improved agriculture with iron plows, and invented paper.
Tang Dynasty	Developed systems of taxation, invented block printing, and established the Tang Code.
Tang Code	A code of laws and punishments for crimes that had five hundred articles divided into twelve sections and the sections dealt with specific crimes, such as forgery, tax violations, desecration of sacred places, military and government violations, and family issues.
Song Dynasty	Established a paper money system, the development of a navy, and the invention of gunpowder.
Mongols	A group of people from Mongolia who gained control of China for a brief period of time under the guidance of their leader Kublai Khan.
Ming Dynasty	A dynasty particularly well known for its poetry, painting, music, and decorative arts.
Qing Dynasty	The last imperial dynasty of China, at its height, it was the largest empire in the world.

11: SOUTH ASIA

11.1 INDUS VALLEY CIVILIZATIONS

In this chapter, we are continuing our discussion of the beginnings of civilizations throughout the world. In the Indus Valley, located in what is today Pakistan and India, Neolithic farming communities developed around 8,500 years ago. At one of these, the site of Mehrgarh, people subsisted on wheat, barley, cattle, sheep, and goats (Scarre, 2005). The occupants of the site lived in houses made of mud brick that had both living and storage areas. Evidence suggests that people traded surplus products for turquoise, shell, and steatite. People also made ceramic vessels that were used for cooking and storage. In addition, the earliest evidence of cotton comes from this site and suggests that the manufacture of cloth for clothing was an important item for the communities, as well as for trade (Moulherat, 2002). Cotton is native to the Indus Valley and was first cultivated there around 7,000 years ago.

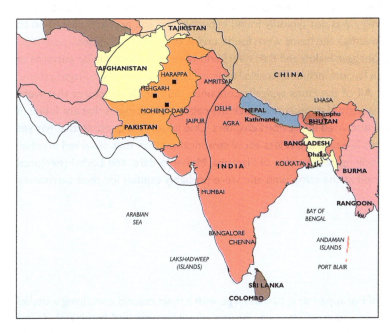

Figure 11-1.

During the Bronze Age, around 4,500 years ago, the Indus Valley civilization (also known as the Harappan civilization) developed. As was the case with the Neolithic communities discussed in Chapter 6, the Indus civilization had excellent resources to rely on, but mineral ores and semiprecious stones were particularly important. Also, the people living in the river valleys developed

Figure 11-2. Indus Valley seals (Image by World Imaging).

irrigation for farming and used coastal areas for collecting fish and shellfish. The coastal areas would also have been places to launch ships for trade. Wheat, barley, and cotton continued to be important crops. Cattle became more dominant and elephants were domesticated for labor and ivory (Sukumar, 2003). Trade was also a crucial part of the economy and people of the Indus Valley traded with surrounding groups for gold, silver, copper, and turquoise.

The Harappans used a pictographic script that has yet to be deciphered. The script was mostly recorded on seals made of clay, stone, bronze, and gold (Figure 11-2). Unlike Mesopotamia and Egypt, the symbols are usually very short inscriptions and had iconographic motifs. The motifs were often animals (such as bulls, elephants, or tigers), mythical animals (a unicorn), or human figures that may represent deities (Chazan, 2011). In addition to the script for recording information, the Harappans also had a system for weights and measures. This was mostly used to measure agricultural items, as a means of calculating taxes, and for trade. For example, each weight unit was approximately one ounce and went from .05 of a unit to 500 units.

The Harappans were also skilled artisans and made a variety of items from clay, bronze, gold, silver, and other materials. Items made from clay include pottery statues, often representing young women moving or dancing. Plates made of copper, bronze, or gold were found in some of the houses in the cities. Jewelry, including bracelets, short and long necklaces, rings, earrings, hair ornaments, and pins, was also found in the cities. Unlike other civilizations that we have discussed, this jewelry was not typically found in burials, but was probably passed on to relatives at the time of death. Although sometimes the items were found under the floors of houses.

The earliest cities developed along the Ghaggar-Hakra and Ravi rivers and were built along similar patterns of organization and layout (Scarre, 2005). These layouts included streets laid in grids, plumbing and drainage systems, and households with wells for clean water. All of the cities typically contained mud brick structures that were similar at sites throughout the region. Interestingly, Harappan cities lack the palaces and temples that are found in the cities of other early civilizations that we discussed in previous chapters. One important question that has yet to be answered about Indus Valley civilizations is why there is less social stratification than that observed in other civilizations. We can explore this more by looking at the cities of Harappa, Mohenjo-daro, and Lothal (explored in more detail below), which were all occupied at the same time and were probably capitals for their territories.

11.2 INDUS VALLEY CITIES

An important Indus Valley city was the city of Harappa. Harappa was large with a main mound containing a citadel and a mud-brick wall (Scarre, 2005). The main center of Harappa consists of public wells and bathing platforms that were found in the southern part of the city. The wells and baths were part of a complex drainage and water system for the area. Within the different areas of the city, sections are delineated with walls and gates. These areas have been described as public structures, markets, and workshops, as well as houses. An area, known as the granary, is also part of the city. The granary is constructed of mud brick and consists of a large foundation, divided into rooms or sections. These sections were probably used to store grain and other agricultural products. The city also had streets with extensive drainage systems, which helped move sewage outside of the city and also prevented flooding in the city during the rainy season. As mentioned above, there were public wells and bathing areas located throughout the city. These were probably gathering places to wash, collect water for household use, and wash clothes.

One area of the city is identified as the artisans' quarter (Fagan, 2006). Large quantities of materials used to make pottery, jewelry, and other products were identified in certain areas, suggesting that the artisans' quarter was divided into sections for different types of manufacture. For example, steatite and stone were found in an area that was probably where stone beads were made. Another area had gold and the tools for making jewelry and gold leaf. In addition, other areas were exclusively for manufacturing pottery.

Some sections of the city were set aside for cemeteries. Most of the burials at Indus Valley sites show very little attention to class or status, which is very different from other groups we have talked about. The majority of burials are simple, with individuals wrapped in cotton shrouds and lacking jewelry or other ornamentation. As

Figure 11-3. Dancing girl of Mohenjo-daro.

mentioned above, most jewelry or other personal items were probably passed on to family and friends at the time of death, rather than used as burial offerings. The layout and order of the cities indicates that there was a lot of planning involved in constructing the city and there were many skilled laborers, engineers and artisans involved in that construction.

The site of Mohenjo-daro is another Indus valley city that was excavated in the 20th century and is composed of mounds that include mud-brick houses and other structures (Singh, 2008). The houses of Mohenjo-daro are rectangular and spread out along streets arranged in a grid pattern. It is estimated that the city housed over 35,000 residents. Archaeologists identified two main sections to the city: the Citadel and the lower part of the city. The Citadel is composed of a multi-chambered mud-brick structure, that is almost 40 feet in height. This structure contained public baths, residences, and large gathering places. In addition, the city had a marketplace, a granary, artisans' workshops, and housing. Artifacts found at the site include statues, seals for making written communications, weights, jewelry, tools, and other items. One of the statues from Mohenjo-daro is known as the "dancing girl," a bronze statue of a young girl (Figure 11-3). These figures have captured the imagination of archaeologists and historians, because the dancing figures are both beautifully made and probably depict real people, because each is unique.

The area of the site known as the "Great Bath" includes a courtyard with steps that lead to a brick pool and is probably the earliest public water container in the world (Figure 11-4). The tank itself measures approximately 40 feet north–south and 20 feet wide and was up to eight feet deep. It is composed of thousands of mud bricks that are sealed with bitumen, a type of tar found in the natural environment. In addition to steps into the pool, there were areas around the side that probably held wooden benches or planks. The role of the Great Bath in Mohenjo-daro society has been debated. Some argue it was simply a public gathering area, while others argue that it had ritual and religious significance (Singh, 2008). Those who believe it had ritual significance suggest that the rooms and structures adjacent to the baths housed priests.

Lothal was another important city of the Indus Valley civilization and was discovered and excavated in the mid-20th century (Singh, 2008). The site was first occupied around 4,400 years ago and was a significant port city for the Harappans. Initially, Lothal was a small fishing village, the Harappans saw the strategic significance of the city, so they expanded it. This is similar to the expansion of cities that we discussed previously, such as Harappa and Mohenjo-daro. The town was built from mud bricks and included a citadel, public baths, and houses. It also featured a prominent market area. By far, the most important aspect of the site was the docks with adjacent storage areas. The location of the city on the Sabarmati River and the Arabian Sea made it important in trade for the rest of the Harappan civilization. The docks were large stone structures that were built to deal with changes in tide and the differing levels of the Sabarmati River. Workshops that made copper, shell, and ivory artifacts were located near the docks.

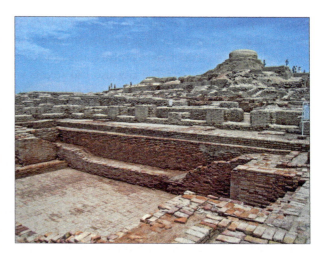

Figure 11-4. Great Bath at Mohenjo-daro (Image by Grjatoi).

Copper ore was brought in to manufacture many different kinds of tools, such as wood-working items, jewelry, fishing equipment, and weapons. Shell was used mostly to create beads, game pieces, and vessels. Ivory was carved into a wide array of products, including game pieces, weights, combs, and jewelry. The workshops outside of the docks contain both the raw materials and the finished items, suggesting that the city both imported the raw materials for production and exported finished artifacts. In particular, the copper ore has been sourced as far away as Arabia (Singh, 2008). This highlights the importance of the Indus Valley in trade routes of the region.

The cities of the Harappan civilization began to decline around 3,800 years ago, when the area became decentralized and the cities largely abandoned. There are several theories as to why this occurred, including invasion, tectonic activity, or climate change (Scarre, 2005). It is most likely that climate change affected the agriculture of the area, because the climate became cooler and drier. The rainy season was less reliable, which affected the growing season. However, it is probable that many factors caused the decline of Harappan culture, and we know that eventually it was replaced by other civilizations in India.

11.5. MAURYA

In the Indus valley, around 2,500 years ago, there were at least 16 different kingdoms that controlled certain territories throughout India. However, a civilization known as the Maurya was founded around 2,300 years ago and spread throughout the Indian subcontinent. The Mauryan civilization was founded by Chandragupta Maurya (Singh, 2008) and he and his descendants eventually controlled an empire that encompassed over five million square miles and was the largest empire in the world at the time. At its height, the empire probably had a population of 30 million, which might not seem like a lot in this day, but it was an immense population over 2,000 years ago. The Mauryan civilization was the first in India to unify all of the kingdoms and territories and control them under one government. The first ruler, Chandragupta Maurya, did many things to unify the empire, including establishing a single currency, setting up four regional governors, organizing the army, and setting up units to collect taxes and organize public works.

Another great ruler of the Maurya civilization was Ashoka, also known as Ashoka the Great (Singh, 2008). He established a treaty with people to the north, so that the Khyber Pass was made safe for trade. He also ruled for over forty years and was initially a very war-like ruler. After a particularly devastating battle to gain control of Kalinga in eastern Indian, he apparently had a complete change of heart and adopted Buddhism. He is also responsible for making the harming of cattle in India illegal. In addition, he banned hunting, violent sports, and slavery (Singh, 2008). Following Ashoka's death in 2,200 years ago, his descendants ruled and the kingdom was not as powerful. After the end of the Mauryan civilization, there was a 600 year period of invasion and influence by cultures outside of India. By about 1700 years ago, an empire known as the Gupta gained control of the empire. This empire changed the religious focus of the people to Hinduism, but continued to emphasize trade as a major part of the empire. However, by 1400 years ago, the empire became weak and much of India separated into smaller, independent states.

11.6. BRINGING IT TOGETHER

The Indian subcontinent has a fascinating history of development. Beginning around 8,500 years ago, early Neolithic villages developed and established permanent villages and agriculture. Neolithic people subsisted on wheat, barley, cattle, sheep, and goats and lived in mud-brick homes. Around 4,500 years ago, at the start of the Bronze Age, a civilization developed in east-central Indian called the Harappan of Indus Valley Civilization. People of the Indus Valley civilization continued to rely on wheat, barley, and cattle, but resources such as mineral ores and trade routes became increasingly important. They also used a pictographic script that has remained undeciphered and developed a uniform set of weights and measures.

The Harappans were also skilled artisans and made a variety of items from clay, bronze, gold, silver, and other materials. Their cities, including Harappa, Mohenjo-daro, and Lothal were constructed following similar patterns of organization and layout. These layouts included streets laid out in grids, plumbing, drainage systems, and wells. Houses and other structures were made from mud brick. Unlike other cities that we have discussed so far, Harappan cities did not have large palaces and temples. Eventually the Indus Valley civilization declined, perhaps due to outside forces or climate change, and was replaced by other kingdoms. One of these kingdoms, the Maurya civilization, originating in western India and ultimately gained power over the Indian subcontinent and became the largest empire of its time. The Maurya civilization established a single government, with four regional governors, unified the military, and established an integrated monetary system. After the death of Ashoka the Great at the end of the Iron Age, the Maurya empire declined and there was a period of about 600 years with outsider influence and control. The Gupta empire briefly regained control from about 1700–1400 years ago, but eventually much of India split into independent states with their own governments.

Key Terms and Concepts

Mehrgarh	A Neolithic village that was established around 8,500 years ago and the occupants subsisted on wheat, barley, cattle, sheep, and goats.
Cotton	Native to the Indus Valley and was first cultivated there around 7,000 years ago.

Indus Valley civilization	Established in east-central India around 4,500 years ago (also known as the Harappan civilization or Harappans).
Indus Valley writing	The Harappans used a pictographic script that has yet to be deciphered and was mostly recorded on seals made of clay, stone, bronze, and gold.
Indus Valley cities	Harappa, Mohenjo-daro, and Lothal were occupied at the same time and were probably capitals for their territories.
Harappa	An Indus Valley city that consists of a main mound with a citadel and a mud-brick wall. There are also large public wells and public bathing platforms.
The Citadel	A monumental structure in Mohenjo-daro that is composed of mud bricks, is almost 40 feet high, and contains public baths, residences, and places for large groups to gather.
Mohenjo-daro	An Indus Valley city that is very similar to Harappa. The city is composed of mounds that include mud-brick houses and immense brick walls. It is estimated that the city housed over 35,000 residents.
The "Great Bath"	An area in Mohenjo-daro that includes a courtyard with steps that lead to a brick pool and is probably the earliest public water container in the world.
Lothal	An important city of the Indus Valley civilization that was discovered and excavated in the mid-20th century, it was first occupied around 4,400 years ago and was an important port city for the Harappans.
Mauryan civilization	An Iron Age civilization that began around 2,300 years ago in India and eventually encompassed over five million square kilometers and was the largest empire in the world at the time.
Chandragupta Maurya	Founder of the Maurya civilization who adopted Buddhism as the central religion for the Mauryan civilization.
Ashoka the Great	A great ruler of the Maurya civilization, he conquered large territories, but eventually converted to Buddhism and passed rules that outlawed fighting, slavery, and harming animals.
Gupta empire	A period from about 1700 to 1400 years ago where India was centralized and the religious emphasis switched to Hinduism.

12: NORTH AMERICA

12.1 ARCHAIC PERIOD

In Chapter 4, we discussed the arrival of humans in the "New World," or the Americas, and that the earliest people in North America were known as the Paleoindians. We also discussed that the end of the Pleistocene (or Ice Age) resulted in a lot of changes to the climate, fauna, and flora of the Americas. Specifically, the climate became warmer, some large-bodied animals (such as mammoth and mastodons) died off, and plant habitats changed. The period that begins after the end of the Pleistocene is known as the Holocene. During the Holocene period people continued to live as hunters and gatherers, but there was increased diversity in the plants and animals they consumed. The early part of the Holocene period is known as the Archaic period and is characterized by people who used stone tools, were nomadic, and subsisted by hunting and gathering, but over time became increasingly complex.

The Archaic period begins roughly around 10,000 years ago and people at this time were adjusting to more temperate conditions. While there was variation in local environments, most groups hunted deer, turkey, rabbits, and squirrel, and collected wild seeds and nuts. Most sites were located along river systems, but some localized camps in upland areas have been documented. One important Early Archaic site is the site of Koster, Illinois, located along the Illinois River and dating to 9,000 years ago. Koster is significant because there is excellent preservation of organic remains and it was occupied sequentially for over 5,000 years (Struever et al., 2000). The Koster site contained abundant animal remains—particularly deer, but also fish and small mammals. Plant remains are a significant source of food for the Koster people as well. As we have discussed for other areas of the world, the focus on plant remains, often results in the domestication of plants. Another aspect of the site is that it also has the earliest dog burials in the Americas, dating to 8,500 years ago. A total of four dog burials were recovered from Koster. This is significant because dogs become an important part of Native American life ways and served people as hunting dogs, companions, pack carriers, and were often buried with humans in the same cemeteries.

An key Early Archaic site in the southeastern U.S. is the site of Dust Cave, Alabama. Initially occupied during the Late Paleoindian period, the site was continuously occupied from 12,500 to 5,600 years ago (Sherwood et al., 2004). Like Koster, the longevity of the occupation of Dust Cave gives archaeologists a chance to observe change over time in the same region. Dust Cave also has excellent preservation of animal and plant remains.

The animals from the site include rabbits, squirrels, waterfowl, turkey, deer and fish (Walker, 1998). Also, there is a huge variety of plants, including hackberry, sumpweed, mayflower, acorn, walnut, and hickory (Hollenbach, 2009). Features from the site indicate that people cooked food in various ways—roasting and using prepared clay surfaces to oven-roast foods and toast nuts and seeds. Other features, dating to around 7,000 years ago, indicate the site was used as a burial site. Similar to Koster, Dust Cave has dog burials. A total of four dog burials have been recovered from the northeast section of the site; the same section of the site that contains human burials (see Figure 5-3). The site probably fulfilled multiple functions, including habitation, cooking, preparing and storing food, as well as burying the dead.

Figure 12-1. Mound A at Poverty Point (Image by Kneimla).

Later in the Archaic period, around 6,000 years ago, some groups began to settle along river systems in the eastern United States and live there for longer periods of time. This is known as the Middle Archaic period. One reason this more semi-sedentary lifestyle may have started is that at this time there was a global drying and warming episode, known as the Hypsithermal. Due to the warming and drying of this period, many river systems stabilized and people could live in the river valleys without fear of flooding. As a result, many groups began to rely on fishing and shellfishing for subsistence. These semi-sedentary sites often resulted in shell middens or mounds, where large piles of shells were deposited. This period is also known as the Shell Mound Archaic (Neusius and Gross, 2007). While initially utilitarian in nature, many of these shell middens became ceremonial sites. For example, in Alabama, Kentucky, and Tennessee, people began to bury their dead in these shell middens.

Some of the most significant shell midden sites of the Archaic period were excavated in the Green River Valley of Kentucky. Sites such as Read and Indian Knoll were large shell midden sites with cemeteries (Neusius and Gross, 2007). During this time, people were still semi-nomadic, but were perhaps becoming more territorial as population size increased. Cemeteries and shell mounds may have been a way to visually mark territories more clearly. Also, during the Middle Archaic period, people became more skilled at making a variety of stone and bone tools. Sites had features used for cooking and storing food, and house structures.

Eventually, some people living in river valleys established large central sites with earthen mound structures. The most prominent of these sites is the site of Poverty Point in Louisiana (Gibson, 2000). This enigmatic site has several mounds, the most notable of which is the "bird"-shaped Mound A (Figure 12-1). Mound A is at the apex of six concentric semi-circular rings that open on a plaza above the Bayou Marcon River. The site is unusual for its size and complexity, because, as far as we know, the occupants did not have agricultural as a subsistence base. It seems that hunting, gathering, and more importantly, fishing were the main sources of food. In addition to the tremendous amount of work that went into building the mounds, there were also many items that were not subsistence related. These include clay items in the shape of birds and artifacts made from copper and galena. Poverty Point was abandoned around 2,700 years ago and other mound-building cultures emerged throughout the Midwest and Southeast.

12.2 AGRICULTURE, SEDENTISM, AND MOUNDS

While not universal throughout the Americas, in many areas, people began to domesticate plants in the Americas. This period is known as the Woodland period and dates to between 3,000 and 1,000 years ago. It is characterized by increased sedentism, horticulture of native plants (such as sumpweed, maygrass, sunflower, gourds, and squash), increased use of pottery, and expansion of mound building. One of the earliest Woodland cultures in Midwestern America is known as the Adena Culture. The Adena are best known for their sedentary, agricultural society, large villages, large burial mounds, and elaborate burial goods.

Some of the most elaborate funerary objects in North America were made by Adena people. These include copper artifacts, ceremonial knives and axes, sheets of mica carved into animal and human figures, stone pipes, pottery, and stone tablets (Neusius and Gross, 2007). These objects were buried with human remains in conical-shaped burial mounds. The individuals in these mounds were high-status individuals, probably chiefs or shamans (religious leaders). These mounds were located near sedentary villages that were scattered throughout the Ohio River Valley.

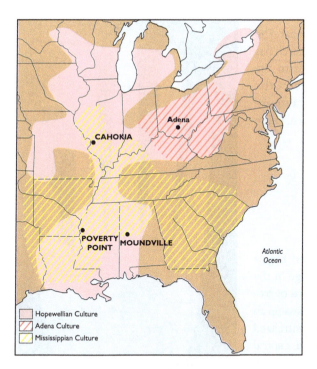

Figure 12-2. Map of the eastern United States showing the locations of some key mount building sites.

Following the Adena Culture, around 2,200 years ago, is the fluorescence of the Hopewell Culture. This culture had many similarities to the Adena and probably grew out of that tradition. However, the Hopewell culture was more widespread and had more elaborate artifacts and burial mounds. Centered initially in the Ohio River Valley, the Hopewell culture spread to encompass the Great Lakes, Northeast, and midsouth, and became known as the Hopewell Interaction Sphere (Neusius and Gross, 2007). The most complex Hopewell ceremonial sites are in the Scioto Valley, Ohio. The sites were utilized as both religious and political centers and included burial mounds and earthworks. Some sites covered up to 100 acres. Similar to sites that we have discussed previously, such as Stonehenge, these Hopewell ceremonial centers did not have yearlong village occupations associated in proximity to them. They usually consisted of multiple burial mounds that contained log tombs with human skeletons and burial goods. The burial goods were usually made from raw materials not found in the local area. For example, copper and galena came from the Great Lakes region, obsidian was from Wyoming, and marine shell was imported from both the Atlantic and Gulf coasts. Some of the best-known artifacts are carved from sheets of mica, such as this hand from the Hopewell Mound Group, Ohio (Figure 12-3).

The "type" site of the Hopewell Culture is the Hopewell Mound Group. The site covers approximately 130 acres and includes two earthen walls, one in the shape of a parallelogram (a four-sided shape with parallel sides offset from each other) and the other in the shape of a square. Inside the walls are one circular earthwork, a D-shaped earthwork, and approximately 30 burial mounds. Another elaborate earthwork site is Newark Earthworks in the Ohio River Valley. The Newark Earthworks covers the largest area of any earthwork in the Americas, over 3,000 acres. These earthworks include three main areas: the Great Circle, the Octagon, and the Wright Earthworks (Neusius and Gross, 2007). The Great Circle is over one thousand feet in diameter and is an eight-foot-high wall surrounding a five-foot-deep moat. The Octagon is over three thousand feet in diameter and research has suggested the center point of the Octagon corresponds to the northern point of the moon's rising at the end of its 18.6 year orbit (Hively and Horn, 2006). The Wright Earthworks includes a square enclosure and parallel banks that lead to an oval enclosure. These earthworks encompass an area of about 20 acres.

12.3 MISSISSIPPIAN SOCIETIES

Following the Woodland period, the Mississippian period begins around 1,000 years ago and lasts until about 500 years ago in the Midwestern and Southeastern United States. It is a culture of tremendous social complexity in eastern North America. Mississippian people were organized into large "city-states" that had centralized governments, priests, and militaries. The city-states had central areas with platform earthen mounds (flat-topped mounds), elaborate earthen burial mounds, and open central plazas surrounded by residential areas and agricultural fields (Neusius and Gross, 2007). Excavations of the platform mounds have revealed they were likely built and then added on to over several hundred years. There is also evidence of house structures on top of the mounds, which

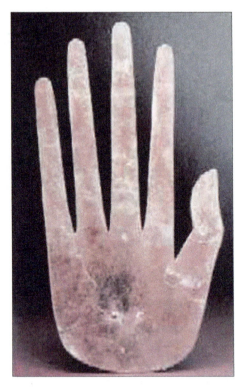

Figure 12-3. Mica hand from the Hopewell Mound Group.

may have been where the chief lived, or areas for performing religious rituals, or both. The burial mounds were for high-status individuals and often contained thousands of elaborate artifacts, as well as the remains of individuals sacrificed to be interred with the high-status individuals. The open plazas were probably for religious rituals, playing games, and large group gatherings. Some of these "downtown" areas were also surrounded by wooden walls or palisades.

Etowah Mounds, in Georgia, is a Mississippian site with these characteristics. Located along the Etowah River, the Etowah site has three large platform mounds at the center of the site. The largest, Mound A, is over 60 feet high and covers three acres, and had several structures built on the mound. The mound area of the site was surrounded by a wood palisade and moat, which may have been for defensive purposes. The burial mounds at Etowah contained copper artifacts, weapons, effigy ceramic vessels with animal and bird figures, clay figurines, and stone statues. The stone statues were of both men and women and were usually found in pairs. Much of the material found in the burial mounds was acquired by trade, including shells from the Gulf Coast, mica and flint from Tennessee, and greenstone and marble for manufacturing the statues from the Carolinas.

Another Mississippian city-state is the site of Moundville, Alabama, located along the Black Warrior River in west-central Alabama. The site originally covered over 300 acres and may have been home to as many as 12,000 people. Multiple platform mounds are located in the city center, with the largest two being mounds A and B. Mound A was almost 60 feet tall and had structures on top. The other mounds also had structures and ranged in height from ten feet to fifty feet. In addition to the platform mounds, several burial mounds and a central plaza are located in the center of the site. This center is surrounded by a wooden palisade.

Artifacts recovered from the site are similar to those found at Etowah and other Mississippian sites. The types of artifacts and the style of the artifacts spread over the Midwest and Southeast has been called the Southeastern Ceremonial Complex (Neusius and Gross, 2007). In addition to raw materials brought in from long distances, commonalities are found in the styles of the artifacts. Designs showing hands with an eye in the center, forked eyes, crosses in circles, striped poles, and bi-lobed arrow are all common motifs in Mississippian artifact designs (Pauketat, 2004). Animal figures are also prominent in the Southeastern Ceremonial Complex, including birds and bird/human figures, spiders, snakes, and panthers. These ceremonial motifs represent complex cosmology and ritual for the Mississippian people.

Figure 12-4. Monk's Mound, Cahokia (Image by QuartierLatin1968).

The largest earthen mound complex in the Americas is Cahokia, located in East St. Louis, Illinois, located on Cahokia Creek. In addition to being the largest earth mound complex, Cahokia was also the largest prehistoric city north of Mexico, with a population of tens of thousands of people in the center and outlying areas (Pauketat, 2009). First occupied around 1,300 years ago, the peak of the construction and population was around 1,000 years ago. The center of the city includes multiple platform and burial mounds, residential structures, and a central plaza. This area is surrounded by a wooden palisade and the city center is shaped like a diamond with a walled interior. Also located inside the central core is a "Woodhenge." This circular wooden henge was constructed of red cedar posts and was rebuilt several times. Several of the posts align with solar solstices and equinoxes, which indicate it may have been used as an astronomical observatory, but also could have been a ceremonial site.

The largest platform mound is known as Monk's Mound and was originally about 100 feet in height and covered 16 acres (Figure 12-4). It is estimated that it took over 21,000,000 cubic feet of earth to build Monk's Mound, which, unlike other platform mounds, has two tiers. Both tiers had structures on them. Another impressive mound in the city center of Cahokia is Mound 72, which is a conical burial mound. Mound 72 contained the remains of over 250 individuals. The person buried at the center of the mound was an adult male, laid out on thousands of shell beads, and interred with artifacts such as projectile points, ceramics, copper artifacts, and other materials. The other remains were most likely sacrificed to be interred with this high-status individual and the human remains include a pit with four headless, adult males, a pit with 52 women of around the same age (early 20s) buried together, and another pit of over 40 individuals who appear to have died violently.

Occupation of Cahokia began to decline around 700 years ago and the site was abandoned by 500 years ago. There are many different theories as to why the site declined and some explanations include deforestation, diminished soil fertility, over-hunting, and warfare as possibilities. Deforestation is very likely given the number of houses and the need for firewood; in addition, the wooden palisade surrounding the city was estimated to have incorporated over 15,000 trees and was rebuilt three times (Pauketat, 2009). The large numbers of people in the area may also have put a strain on the natural resources, such as animals for protein and arable land for agriculture. In general, most Mississippian sites were abandoned by the time Europeans arrived in the early 16th century, which prompted many Europeans to wonder who had built the mounds.

In the northeastern United States, sites had large populations, numerous houses, and were palisaded, but did not have the large burial and platform mounds associated with the Mississippian Culture and also did not have artifacts representing the Southeastern Ceremonial Complex. However, beginning around 1,000 years ago, there is maize, beans, and squash agriculture, and settlement into more permanent villages. The villages typically had long houses that probably contained multiple families. Ceramics had complex incised designs and were used for cooking, storage, and ceremonial activities. In addition to agriculture, people also probably hunted, fished, and gathered nuts to supplement their diets. Complex socio-political interactions and conflict over territory may also have led to warfare between villages. Some of these Woodland populations eventually became known as the Iroquois confederacy in historic times and included seven tribes.

12.4. SOUTHWEST COMPLEXITY

In the southwestern United States, agriculture that was centered on corn, beans, and squash began around 4,000 years ago. As populations increased, three main groups developed, including the Hohokam in southern Arizona, the Anasazi in the Four Corners area, and the Mogollon in central Arizona. These cultures subsisted on corn, bean, and squash agriculture that required irrigation, developed complex ceramic styles, and, in some cases, built large cities. The Hohokam Culture was centered in the low desert, which had seasonal rainfall, thus requiring irrigation canals from rivers for their fields. The site of Snaketown is a Hohokam site located on the Gila and Salt rivers. Occupation began around 1,700 years ago and people lived in pithouses, which were semi-subterranean, circular structures. The population of Snaketown probably reached its peak around 1,100 years ago with a population of over 1,000 people living in over 100 pithouses (Neusius and Gross, 2007). The site includes a central courtyard or plaza, several public structures, and a ball court. The ball court was a large, semi-subterranean area with sloped sides. They are similar in size and shape to ball courts found in Mesoamerica, prompting theories that some southwestern groups had contact with Mesoamerican groups over time. The ball courts in Mesoamerica are used to play a ball game that was both a sport and a ritual event. Around 900 years ago, Snaketown was abandoned, which may be related to a series of droughts that occurred around that time (Fagan, 2009).

Another complex southwestern culture is the Anasazi (also known as Ancestral Puebloans) who lived in the Four Corners area around 800 years ago. The Anasazi are known for their adobe structures located in cliff walls. Like the Hohokam, they also grew corn, beans, and squash, and used irrigation to channel seasonal flood waters to agricultural fields. One area of Anasazi occupation is Chaco Canyon, New Mexico, which was occupied between 1,100 and 900 years ago. The canyon is over 25,000 square miles and includes multiple towns, roads, and irrigation systems. Also, evidence can be seen of trade in turquoise that came from over 100 miles

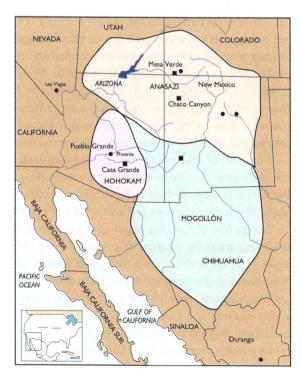

Figure 12-5. Map of the southwestern United Stats showing the Four Corners area.

away and was manufactured into beads that were traded south into Mexico.

Pueblo Bonito is the best-known town of Chaco Canyon and included pithouses, kivas (circular, ceremonial structures), and multi-level structures (Neusius and Gross, 2007). Pueblo Bonito may have been only periodically occupied and largely used as a ceremonial city, given the large number of ceremonial kivas (including several very large kivas, known as "Great Kivas"). Another town in Chaco Canyon is Chetro Ketl. Chetro Ketl contained as many as 500 rooms that were five stories high in some cases and also had over ten kivas. The multi-story homes had wooden beams to support the adobe structures. All of the towns were connected in Chaco Canyon by a series of roads. In addition, communities on the outside of the canyon were connected by road systems. These probably linked the communities as well as provided easier routes for trade, but may have also served a ceremonial purpose in connecting the locations of kivas.

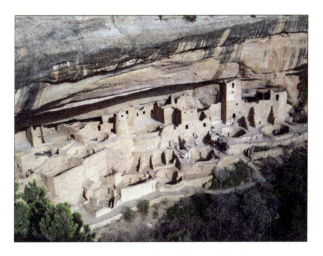

Figure 12-6. Cliff Palace, Mesa Verde National Park (Image by Staplegunther at en.wikipedia).

Mesa Verde, Colorado, is another area of Anasazi occupation. Beginning around 1,500 years ago, people began to settle in this area to grow crops and eventually built towns in cliffs. The structures were multi-level and were made from sandstone, mortar, and wooden beams. Cliff Palace is one of the largest of these and includes 220 rooms and 23 kivas, as well as ceremonial temples (Figure 12-6). Spruce House had 130 rooms and eight kivas. Square Tower House has the tallest structure in Mesa Verde, over four stories high. All of the cliff towns were accessed by climbing ladders or by toe-holds carved into the cliff face. Not all people in Mesa Verde lived in cliff dwellings, as there is evidence of structures in the valley floor, but they would have been important for defensive purposes.

The Mogollon Culture evolved in the southwestern corner of New Mexico and extended into Arizona and southward into northern Mexico (Neusius and Gross, 2007). The Mogollon were originally small, nomadic groups who lived in mountainous parts of the area. After corn and bean agriculture was introduced to the area, people constructed villages that included pithouses and kivas—similar to the Hohokam and Anasazi cultures. Mogollon burials were not elaborate and people were typically buried in shallow pits in the floors of houses or in refuse middens outside the villages. The Mogollon are also well known for their ceramics, with bowls painted in black with a white background and featuring abstract designs, animals, and human figures.

The regions occupied by the Hohokam, Anasazi, and Mogollon eventually became abandoned around 700 to 500 years ago. Analysis of human remains indicates malnutrition and disease were increasing around this time and there was increased evidence of warfare. Climate change may have been part of the reason the area was abandoned, due to a period of drought occurring around this time that would have made growing crops difficult. Some research has suggested there is evidence of cannibalism at sites in Chaco Canyon, which may indicate starvation or violence from outside groups (Turner, 1992). Cannibalism is highly controversial and the Puebloan descendants of the Anasazi reject claims of cannibalism.

12.5. BRINGING IT TOGETHER

After the end of the Pleistocene epoch, the climate became warmer and this began what is known as the Holocene epoch. Archaeologically, this period is called the Archaic and is characterized by mobile hunter-gatherers traveling over large areas. People began to rely more heavily on collecting seeds and nuts, in addition to hunting and fishing. Some important Archaic sites include Koster and Dust Cave, which were occupied during the Early Archaic period. Middle Archaic sites, such as Read and Indian Knoll were located in the Green River Valley of Kentucky and were areas of intensive shellfish collecting. The Late Archaic site of Poverty Point has mound structures, a plaza, and artifacts traded from long distances, indicating an increased social complexity. The Woodland period is distinguished by a dependence on cultivated plants, such as sumpweed, maygrass, sunflowers, and squash. In addition, people began to live in sedentary villages and used pottery for cooking and storage. Some sites in the Midwest, built by the Adena and Hopewell cultures, consisted of large earthworks and elaborate burial mounds. In the Mississippian period, population size increased tremendously in areas of the Midwest and Southeastern United States. City-states developed in some areas that were controlled by independent leaders. These city-states usually contained large platform mounds, open plazas, conical burial mounds, and palisades. Maize, beans, and squash replaced many early plant domesticates. The Mississippian culture also probably shared common religious beliefs that were expressed in the artifacts of the Southeastern Ceremonial Complex.

In the southwestern United States, agriculture occurred earlier than in the east, around 4,000 years ago. Three cultures in the southwest shared many commonalities, including large villages, irrigation agriculture, extensive trade networks, pithouses, and kivas. The Hohokam, located in southern Arizona, had many villages, but the largest was at Snaketown and contained hundreds of pithouses, multiple kivas, and extensive irrigation canals. The Anasazi were located in the Four Corners region and had multiple settlements in Chaco Canyon and Mesa Verde. Some of the settlements were located in cliffs and contained multi-storied houses made from stone and timber. Finally, the Mogollon were from southwestern New Mexico and Arizona and northern Mexico. This culture is probably best known for their black-on-white pottery. At around 700–500 years ago, many of these sites were abandoned, and while theories differ on the reasons behind abandonment, it may have been due to drought conditions that would no longer support intensive agriculture.

Key Terms and Concepts

Holocene epoch	A period beginning around 10,000 years ago at the end of the Ice Age, was much warmer than the Pleistocene.
Archaic period	Period from 10,000 years ago to around 3,000 years ago and characterized by hunter-gatherers who became increasingly dependent on plants.
Koster site	An Early Archaic site in Illinois. The earliest dog burials in the Americas, dating to 8,500 years ago, were recovered from this site.
Dust Cave	A Late Paleoindian to Early Archaic site in Alabama that contained abundant stone tools, and plant and animal remains. Also contains dog and human burials.
Hypsithermal	A warming period occurring around 8,000 to 5,000 years ago.

Shell Mound Archaic	A phenomenon in some river valley and coastal sites where groups relied very heavily on shellfish resources for at least part of the year.
Poverty Point	A Late Archaic site in Louisiana whose inhabitants relied heavily on fishing and plant collecting and built several mounds, some formed into concentric rings and one shaped like a bird in flight.
Woodland period	Beginning around 3,000 years ago when many groups shifted to cultivating plants, living in sedentary villages, making pottery, and constructing burial mounds.
Adena culture	Centered mostly in Ohio, Adena people built earthworks and burial mounds and constructed non-utilitarian artifacts out of exotic materials.
Hopewell culture	A later iteration of the Adena culture, but more widespread and with more extensive earthworks, wider trade networks, and elaborate burial mounds.
Mississippian period	Beginning around 1,000 years ago in the Midwestern and Southeastern United States, people began to cultivate corn, beans, and squash intensively, build large cities with platform mounds, burial mounds, plazas, and palisades.
Etowah Mound	A Mississippian period city in Georgia.
Moundville	A Mississippian period city in Alabama.
Southeastern Ceremonial Complex	Designs and motifs represented in artifacts that may indicate socio-political and religious concepts of the Mississippian period.
Cahokia	The largest Mississippian city, located in Illinois, and containing the largest earthen structure in the Americas, multiple elaborate burial mounds, a woodhenge, and a palisade.
Monk's Mound	The largest earthen mound in the Americas, located at Cahokia.
Mound 72	An elaborate burial mound from Cahokia.
Hohokam	A southwestern culture from southern Arizona whose people subsisted on corn, beans, and squash, had irrigated fields, lived in pithouses, and built ceremonial kivas.
Kiva	A circular, semi-subterranean structure used for ceremonial purposes among some southwestern agriculturalists.
Snaketown	A large Hohokam village.

Anasazi	Also known as ancestral Puebloans and located in the Four Corners region of the United States, they practiced irrigation agriculture and built elaborate towns with pithouses, kivas, and multi-storied structures.
Pueblo Bonito	An Anasazi town containing several great kivas and hundreds of pithouses. May have been used as a seasonally occupied ceremonial site.
Chaco Canyon	Occupied by the Anasazi with many towns, roads, and agricultural fields.
Cliff houses	Large settlements in Chaco Canyon that were located in rockshelters of the canyon and containing multi-storied structures made from stone, mortar, and wood. Examples of cliff houses are Cliff Palace, Spruce House, and Square Tower House.
Mogollon	Located in southern Arizona and New Mexico, a culture very similar to the Hohokam and Anasazi, and known for their detailed black-on-white pottery bowls.

13: MESOAMERICA

13.1 EARLY MESOAMERICA

Mesoamerica is an area of the New World that includes Mexico, Belize, Guatemala, El Salvador, Nicaragua, and Honduras. Similar to North America, Mesoamerica was settled by Paleoindian people during the Ice Age. Hunter-gatherers lived in seasonal camps and moved frequently to take advantage of regional resources. By around 6,000 years ago, many groups had domesticated maize (corn) from a wild plant known as teosinte (Flannery, 1976). Other early domesticates included beans, amaranth, and chili peppers. This period was known as the Formative period and was characterized by permanent villages with wattle and daub structures (wood and mud/clay), the appearance of pottery and specialized crafts, increased social stratification, increased population, increased trade, and the beginnings of a writing system (Flannery, 1976).

One early Mesoamerican village is San Jose Mogote, located in the Valley of Oaxaca and dating to around 3,400 years ago. The site covers around five acres and contains both domestic and public structures (Flannery, 1976). In addition to maize, amaranth, and chili peppers, avocados were also cultivated at San Jose Mogote. Excavations of the structures revealed that they were made from wattle and daub, contained hearths, earth ovens, and

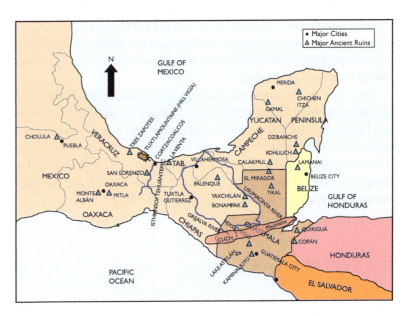

Figure 13-1. Map of Mesoamerica showing ancient sites and modern cities.

Figure 13-2. Colossal Stone Head Monument at San Lorenzo.

stone tools for processing plants, known as manos (hand stones) and metates (bottom stones). Pits dug into the soil were used to store surplus crops and pottery vessels were used for cooking and storage. Craft specialization at San Jose Mogote was focused on producing magnetite mirrors. Magnetite was acquired locally, manufactured into mirrors, and then traded as far away as the Gulf Coast.

Some of the earliest writing also appears at the site of San Jose Mogote in the form of a glyph. Mesoamerican script uses glyphs (images) that represent words or sounds and is often referred to as hieroglyphic writing, but Egyptian hieroglyphics and Mesoamerican script are not related (Coe, 1992; Scarre, 2005). Unlike Egyptian writing, there has not been a Rosetta Stone recovered for Mesoamerican script, so not all Mesoamerican writing has been deciphered. However, it is often depicted on stone monuments and in the Mayan and Aztec periods, discussed below, books called codices recorded religious rituals, dynastic information, and astronomical observations.

At the beginning of the Pre-Classic period, around 3,000 years ago, a culture known as the Olmec exhibited the earliest evidence of emerging political complexity (Evans, 2008). Located in the current area of Vera Cruz, along the Gulf Coast, the Olmec constructed a series of towns that had public architecture and populations of several thousand people. The Olmec people were also known for their art; in particular, the carving of jade and other stone, elaborate ceramic vessels, and mirrors of polished iron ore (Evans, 2008). They are also known for erecting large stone head sculptures (known as colossal stone heads) in their towns that may have represented their leaders (Figure 13-2). The architecture of Olmec towns, such as San Lorenzo, La Venta, and Tres Zapotes, includes basalt tombs, central plazas and ceremonial platforms, and pyramids (Scarre, 2005). However, around 2,400 years ago, the Olmec towns were abandoned, many of the public structures were destroyed, and most of the colossal head monuments were mutilated and pushed over. It is unclear what caused this abandonment, but theories such as political unrest, external pressure, and climate change have been postulated.

Elsewhere in Mesoamerica, the large settlement at Monte Alban, located in the Oaxaca Valley, grew to a population of over 15,000 people by around 2,300 years ago. Known as the first city in Mesoamerica, the site was built on a ridge and included a city center with a central plaza, upper-class residences, stone platforms, and tombs. The site also had a stone wall built around the edge of the ridge. Many of the stone structures show human figures engaged in various activities, including dancing (called the Danzante figures), religious rituals, and conquests. Most of the population lived in houses built at the base of the ridge and there is also evidence of markets and craft specialization areas (Flannery, 1976).

13.2 TEOTIHUACAN

In the Valley of Mexico, near present-day Mexico City, an enormous city developed to cover seven square miles and was home to almost 125,000 people by around 1,500 years ago and was the dominant political structure for the entire basin (Scarre, 2005). Teotihuacan may have grown due to its strategic location and access to natural resources, such as obsidian for trade, springs for fresh water, and rich agricultural land. The site was laid out in a very strict grid pattern with a main street (known as the Avenue of the Dead) that went from north to south and an east-to-west cross street. Pyramids and temples were made from limestone, then faced with lime plaster and painted. One of the main buildings includes the Temple of Quezalcoatl (Temple of the Feathered Serpent), which contained over 200 sacrificial victims buried to consecrate the building.

The pyramids located along the Avenue of the Dead are similar in size and overall shape to Egyptian pyramids, but were made by piling up rubble, then facing it with limestone in a "stepped" pattern,

Figure 13-3. Pyramid of the Sun, Teotihuacan, Mexico.

known as talud-tablero (an architectural style with a flat platform, or the tablero, and a sloped surface, or talud). The largest is the Pyramid of the Sun (Figure 13-3), located on the east side of the Avenue of the Dead, with the staircase facing west and aligned with the setting of the sun during the summer solstice (Evans, 2008). The pyramid was built over a cave that contained offerings, such as ceramic bowls and obsidian. Construction of the pyramid was conducted in two phases, the first completed approximately 1,900 years ago and the second completed around fifty years later, which resulted in an original height of 246 feet (although today it stands around 200 feet high) and a width of 738 feet (Scarre, 2005). The talud-tablero construction was probably covered with plaster and painted, though this has since eroded away. The second-largest structure at Teotihuacan is the Pyramid of the Moon, which was built slightly after the Pyramid of the Sun at the northern apex of the Avenue of the Dead. The pyramid was around 140 feet tall after the fifth and final stage of construction was completed. Associated with this final stage is a burial that includes four human skeletons, animal remains, jewelry, ceremonial vessels, a turquoise mask, and obsidian blades.

Surrounding the ceremonial center of the city are over 2,000 residential structures. Many of these structures are laid out like compounds with houses and storage buildings connected with inner courtyards. Some were so large, they most likely housed up to 100 individuals who were probably related (Scarre, 2005). These buildings had adobe or stone rooms connected with passageways, plaster-lined floors, and drainage systems. In addition to residential buildings, some areas of the site suggest an artisan area where ceramic vessels, statues, turquoise and coral jewelry, and obsidian artifacts were made. Some artifacts from Teotihuacan are found as far away as Guatemala and Belize.

Beginning around 1,400 years ago, the population of Teotihuacan diminished and most construction at the site ceased. Archaeological evidence suggests that some of the central buildings and temples were burned around this time. By around 1,300 years ago, the site was abandoned. Theories for the decline and the abandonment of the city include external causes (warfare), internal strife, and drought. Warfare has been largely ruled out, because it was mainly the structures in the city center that were burned and not surrounding apartments and markets. Internal causes may have been a factor and the destruction is similar to the case of the Olmec Culture, where people may have revolted against the ruling elite. Drought in the area did occur and may have been the reason behind a revolt. In any case, the city was completely empty by the time the Aztecs arrived and hence the name Teotihuacan means "City of the Dead" in the Aztec language, Nahuatl.

13.3 THE MAYA

Mayan cities developed in multiple ecological zones in southern Mesoamerica around 1,800 years ago. The Mayan cities were independent city-states, similar to the Mississippian cities of North America, and each had their own hereditary rulers, priests, armies, merchants, artisans, and farmers. The population was supported by trade and farming. Trade was facilitated by navigable river systems throughout the interior and also movement of goods up and down the Gulf and Pacific coasts. Farming was done by creating wetlands (often by flooding swamps and river floodplains) and planting up to three crops a year. Although the city-states were independent, the Maya shared a common written and spoken language, religion, and sociopolitical systems.

As mention previously, Mayan script is glyphs that represent words and sounds. The Maya developed writing primarily to record the events in the lives of rulers, rituals, and astronomical events. In addition to written script, the Maya also had numbers and a calendar system. Numbers were recorded as an "eye" for zero, a dot for one, and a bar for five. The calendar system (also called the Calendar Round) consisted of two calendars, rotating together. The first was the astronomical calendar, which was 365 days long, composed of 18 months of 20 days each and five extra days at the end of each year. Another other calendar, known as the sacred almanac, was 260 days long and included 20 day names and 13 numbers (Evans, 2008). Each began at the same point, which marked the beginning of a "cycle." The conclusion of each cycle occurred after 52 years when the dates matched up again. When a cycle ended, it was an important event for the Maya and was marked by rituals, sacrifice, and the construction of monuments.

The Maya worshipped many different gods and each day, month, city, and occupation had its own special deity. Some of the more important Mayan deities included Itzamna (the lord of the heavens), Kinich Ahuau (sun god), Chaac (rain god), Yun Kaax (god of corn), Ah Puc (god of death), and Ix Chel (goddess of the moon) (Evans, 2008). There were many different festivals and ceremonies in the Mayan religion and some of the rituals included blood sacrifice. Sometimes the kings would pierce their tongues or foreskin with stingray spines, bleed onto bark paper, and then burn the paper as an offering to the gods. In other cases, sacrifice was more drastic and involved human sacrifice. Some Mayan sculptures and bas-relief carvings on monuments show individuals being decapitated (Evans, 2008).

Another important ritual for the Maya was the ball game. While this game was probably invented in the Olmec region, the Maya incorporated the game into their myth of the "Hero Twins" who played the underworld gods in a ball game and won. The game is usually played in an I-shaped court with a solid rubber ball and between three and five players, though the rules varied throughout Mesoamerica (Scarre, 2005). Stone markers in the center of the ball courts may have been goals, but some ball courts have stone rings on the sides, like hoops in basketball, though the Mayan stone rings were vertical. Players wore special gear (depicted on stone monuments), including belts padded with cotton and helmets. The ball was moved by hitting it with the hips and maneuvering it to the goal. Ball courts are found through Mesoamerica and in some

Figure 13-4. Temple I, Tikal, Guatemala (Image by Raymond Ostertag).

cases the game was probably more of a sport than a ritual ceremony, but there is evidence on some monuments of ball players being decapitated as part of rituals.

There were many important cities of the Classic Mayan Region. One of these was Copan, located in Honduras. It was a large city with two pyramids and a ball court. The pyramid at the north of the city center has a stairway that inscribes the history of the rulers and is called the hieroglyphic staircase. At the base of the staircase is a stela (stone marker) that was dedicated by the fifteenth ruler of Copan ("Smoke Shell") and dated 756 A.D. (Evans, 2008). Another important city was the city of Tikal, located in Guatemala. The city center contains multiple pyramids, palaces, north–south and east–west avenues, royal tombs, and a ball court (Figure 13-4). Tikal covers an area of around six square miles and was home to approximately 60,000 people at its height. It is located today in Tikal National Park, which preserves the city, but is also a nature preserve. The city of Palenque, located in southern Mexico, contains multiple buildings, monuments, temples, tombs, and a ball court. It is best known for the burial of Pacal in the Temple of the Inscriptions. Lord Pacal, whose name means "shield," ruled for 68 years and died at the age of 80. His tomb contained a massive stone coffin carved with Mayan script that celebrated his rule and he was interred with an elaborate jade mask.

Around 1,200 years ago, many of the Maya cities were depopulated and monumental construction ended. By 1,100 years ago, most of the cities were abandoned. Several factors may have caused the collapse including warfare, disease, peasant revolt, and drought. While drought has been well documented in the region at around the time of the Mayan collapse, not all of the cities were abandoned at the same time. Some cities have archaeological evidence to suggest warfare was the cause, some show disease and malnutrition (perhaps associated with the drought) caused a decline, and some sites indicate internal political unrest. It is likely that all of these causes were factors and as cycles of warfare, drought, and disease erupted in the region, it weakened the power of the rulers. The Classic Mayan era cities were abandoned, but outlying villages and agricultural areas continued to be populated into historic times.

After the collapse of the Classic Maya in Southern Mexico, Belize, Guatemala, and Honduras, several cities evolve in the northern Yucatan. This begins the Post-Classic period of Mesoamerica. The largest city in the area is the site of Chichen Itza and it covers an area of five acres (Coe, 1999). The largest structure is named El Castillo, which is a stepped pyramid that is almost 100 feet high and around 180 feet wide at the base (Evans, 2008). Each side has a staircase; at the bottom of the northern staircase is the carved head of a serpent. The pyramid is aligned so that during the setting of the sun on the spring equinox, the sun casts a shadow on the northern staircase that resembles a serpent going down the side of the structure (Figure 13-5). Other structures at Chichen Itza include the Great Ballcourt, which is 551 feet long by 230 feet wide and has two stone rings on the sides of the court. There are also temples, including the Temple of the Warriors and the Temple of a Thousand Columns. Finally, the Sacred Cenote is part of the underground river system in the Yucatan, where frequently "sinks" or "wells" form and the water is accessible from the surface. There are other cenotes at the site that provided fresh water, but the Sacred Cenote contains sacrificial remains, including statues, gold, jade, and human remains.

Figure 13-5. El Casitllo, Chichen Itza, at the spring equinox.

13.4 AZTEC EMPIRE

In central Mexico during Post-Classic times, we see the development of a well-known culture called the Aztec. Prior to the Aztec, however, a group known as the Toltecs lived in the region north of Mexico City between 1,100 and 800 years ago. The capital of the Toltecs was Tula Grande, which covered four square miles with a population of 30,000–60,000 residents (Evans, 2008). The city is characterized as being focused on trade and there are many areas where craftspeople and merchants lived and worked. The city also contained stepped pyramids and structures of columns shaped like warriors called Atlantean figures. Tula Grande was burned and looted 800 years ago, possibly by civil war or conflicts with outside groups, and thus the Toltec empire collapsed.

At around the same time of the collapse of the Toltec, the people known as the Mexica, who originated to the north of Tula, began to move south into the Valley of Mexico. The mythical homeland of the Mexica was Aztlan. The Mexica had a legend that a leader named Tenoch had a vision from the war god Huizilopochtli who told Tenoch to lead his people until he found an eagle sitting on a cactus eating a snake. Once Tenoch found this site, he was to build a great city to honor the gods and the gods in turn would make the Aztec. Thus, the city was called Tenochtitlan and became the capital of the Aztec Empire in A.D. 1325 (Scarre, 2005). Now Mexico City, Tenochtitlan was located on an island in the middle of Lake Texcoco in the Valley of Mexico, and the city was connected to the mainland by a series of causeways. In addition to the causeways, the city had multiple canals that people navigated by canoe. The city center contained a great pyramid known as the Templo Mayor (Figure 13-6). The Templo Mayor had two shrines at the top, one to Huitzilopochtli and one to Tlaloc (the rain god). At the base of the pyramid was a sculpture of Coyolxauhqui (goddess who was leader of the star gods). On either side of the Templo Mayor are pyramids dedicated to the Huitzilopochtli and Tlaloc. In addition to the temples, there were also palaces and a central marketplace known as the Tlateloco. At its height the city was occupied by around 125,000 people and covered five square miles (Scarre, 2005).

The Aztec economy was based on agriculture and trade. The agricultural fields were called chinampas and were artificial islands built up between long, straight drainage canals along the shores of the lake. As the empire expanded (largely through military conquests), tribute from conquered territories was brought into the capital. Each Aztec town had markets and, according to records, they were open on certain days of the month. The Tlateloco, in Tenochtitlan, was probably open every day, however. According to the Spanish conquistador Bernal Diaz del Castillo (who arrived with Cortés in the early 16th century), items exchanged in the market included agriculture products, ceramics, flowers, crafts, dogs (for food), and slaves (1956).

The Aztec kept track of trade and exchange, tribute paid to the rulers, and religious rituals in books called codices. Very few pre-conquest books survived, but there are also records compiled by the Spanish. One of the most famous is the Florentine Codex, which was compiled by the Spanish Priest Bernardo de Sahagun. The Florentine Codex consists of interviews Sahagun

Figure 13-6. Reconstruction of the Tenochtitlan.

carried out with Aztec informants written both in Nahuatl, the native Aztec language, and Spanish (Evans, 2008). The text has twelve chapters, called books, and covers three themes: religion, sociopolitical issues, and natural history. One of the most disturbing things the codex records is the critical role of human sacrifice in Aztec ritual. The Florentine Codex provides detailed descriptions of how sacrifice is carried out and how it varied depending on what god was being honored.

Aztec society was organized with the kings and their families at the top of the hierarchy, then merchants, commoners and slaves in descending order to the bottom of the hierarchy. The records of the rulers begin in A.D. 1376, with a leader called Acamapichtli who ruled until A.D. 1391. The last ruler was Cuauhtemoc, who ruled from A.D. 1520–1525. The ruler at the time of the Spanish arrival was Moctezuma II, who ruled from A.D. 1502–1520, and expanded the empire to its maximum extent (Evans, 2008). Hernán Cortés arrived on the coast of Vera Cruz in A.D. 1519, sent by his cousin, the governor of Cuba, to explore Mexico. At the coast, he was given a female translator named Malinche (she knew Nahuatl and Mayan) who learned Spanish (Evans, 2008). Malinche is known as a traitor in Mexico today due to the help she gave Cortés in conquering Mexico, although some say she saved people by helping Cortés negotiate peacefully with some of the cities they visited. Moctezuma II heard of the Spanish arrival and sent gifts to them. Some scholars think that Moctezuma II may have thought that Cortés was the return of the god Quetzalcoatl (the feather serpent god), who was prophesied to return the same year that Cortés arrived, but other scholars dispute this claim (Restall, 2003). Eventually, Cortés made his way to Tenochtitlan where he was greeted by Moctezuma II and his nobles. At one point, Cortés had to leave the city to deal with another expedition of Spaniards that had arrived at the Coast of Vera Cruz. While he was away, there was fighting in the city between the Spaniards and the Aztec, so Cortés returned. Soon after his return, in A.D. 1520, Moctezuma II was killed (either by his own people or the Spaniards) and the Spanish were forced from the city. Cortés was joined by people from Tlaxcala, who were enemies of the Aztec and together they laid siege to Tenochtitlan. The siege lasted for 85 days and ended when the Spanish captured the northeast section of the city and the last king of the Aztec, Cuauhtemoc, surrendered in A.D. 1521.

13.5. BRINGING IT TOGETHER

Mesoamerica is an area with a rich archaeological history. Beginning around 6,000 years ago, corn was domesticated and people began to settle in sedentary villages. One of the earliest of these villages is San Jose Mogote in the Valley of Oaxaca. Towns soon evolved, particularly in the Olmec area (gulf coast) and took on a characteristic layout with a town center, central plaza, pyramids, temples, stone monuments, and tombs. Some of the Olmec towns include San Lorenzo, La Venta, and Tres Zapotes. These cities often had colossal stone heads that may have been representations of their leaders. In western Mexico, a city called Monte Alban evolved and became home to around 15,000 people. Another large city, located in central Mexico, was Teotihuacan. Teotihuacan covered a large area and the city center included two large pyramids (one pyramid, the Pyramid of the Sun is the largest stone structure in the Americas), temples, tombs, and a central plaza, all connected by a main avenue laid out on a north–south axis. In southern Mexico, the Maya were a group of people who shared common language, writing systems, and religious beliefs. They built large independent city-states that contained pyramids, temples, palaces, tombs, and stone monuments. The Mesoamerican writing system flourished during the Mayan era and the Maya recorded astronomical events, had an advanced calendar system, and also recorded religious rituals and the history of their kings. After the collapse of the Classic Maya 1,100 years ago, large cities evolved in the northern Yucatan, including Chichen Itza, which has a large, astronomically aligned pyramid (known as El Castillo) and a ball court. In central Mexico, the Toltec Culture flourished beginning around 1,100 years ago and they built their capital, Tula Grande, in the Lerma and Tula river valleys. The Toltec were replaced by people from the north, known as the Mexica initially, but who later became the Aztec. The Aztec built a capital city in the valley of Mexico called Tenochtitlan, which had great temples to their war god and rain god and ruled over a vast territory covering much of northern and eastern Mexico. Despite their great power, in A.D. 1521, the Aztec people were conquered by the Spanish led by Hernán Cortés and Mexico became a Spanish ruled colony. Though, the Aztec live on in the modern Mexican people through language, culture, and traditions.

Key Terms and Concepts

Mesoamerica	Is an area of the New World that roughly includes Mexico, Belize, Guatemala, El Salvador, Nicaragua, and Honduras.
Maize	Corn domesticated from a wild plant known as teosinte.
San Jose Mogote	An early Mesoamerican village, located in the Valley of Oaxaca and known for its production of magnetite mirrors.
Olmec	A culture known to exhibit the earliest evidence of emerging political complexity, located in the current area of Vera Cruz, along the Gulf Coast of Mexico.
San Lorenzo, La Venta, and Tres Zapotes	Olmec towns.
Colossal Head Monuments	Large basalt carvings of human heads, thought to represent Olmec leaders.
Monte Alban	A city in the Valley of Oaxaca.
Teotihuacan	A city located near the Valley of Mexico that covered seven square miles and was home to almost 125,000 people by around 1,500 years ago.
Talud-tablero	Mesoamerican method for constructing pyramids that involved piling up rubble and then facing it with limestone in a "stepped" pattern.
Pyramid of the Sun	Located on the east side of Teotihuacan, the pyramid's staircase faces east and aligns with the setting of the sun during the summer solstice. The tallest stone pyramid in the Americas.
City-states	Independent Mayan cities had their own hereditary rulers, priests, armies, merchants, artisans, and farmers.
Mesoamerican script	Uses glyphs (images) that represent words or sounds.

Mayan Calendar System	A calendar system (also called the Calendar Round) that consisted of two calendars, rotating together, called the sacred almanac (260 days) and the astronomical year (365 days).
Mesoamerican ball game	A game that is usually played in an I-shaped court with a solid rubber ball and between three and five players, though the rules varied throughout Mesoamerica. Stone markers in the center of the ball courts may have been goals, but some ball courts have stone rings on the sides.
Copan	A Mayan city, located in Honduras that contains a large pyramid, which has a stairway that inscribes the history of the rulers and is called the hieroglyphic staircase.
Tikal	A Mayan city, located in Guatemala that contains multiple pyramids, palaces, north–south and east–west avenues, royal tombs, and a ball court.
Palenque	A Mayan city, located in southern Mexico, which contains multiple buildings, monuments, temples, tombs, and a ball court.
Pacal	Lord of Palenque, he ruled for 68 years and died at the age of 80; his tomb is in the Temple of Inscriptions.
Chichen Itza	A Post-Classic city in the Yucatan, Mexico, that covers an area of five acres and has a large pyramid (named El Castillo) that is almost 100 feet high and around 180 feet wide at the base.
Toltecs	A culture located in the Tula and Lerma river valleys north of Mexico City.
Tula Grande	The capital of the Toltecs, which covered four square miles with a population of 30,000–60,000.
Mexica	Originated in northern Mexico and eventually moved south to form the Aztec civilization.
Aztlan	Mythical homeland of the Mexica.
Tenoch	An Aztec leader who had a vision from the war god Huizilopochtli, who sent him on a quest to find an eagle sitting on a cactus eating a snake where he founded the city Tenochtitlan in honor of the gods.
Tenochtitlan	Capital of the Aztecs with a main temple (called the Templo Mayor) that had two shrines at the top, one to Huitzilopochtli and one to Tlaloc (the rain god).
Tlateloco	The marketplace in Tenochtitlan.

The Florentine Codex	A book by the priest Sahagun that consists of interviews with Aztec informants written both in Nahuatl, the native Aztec language, and Spanish.
Moctezuma II	The ruler at the time of the Spanish arrival who ruled from A.D. 1502 to 1520.
Hernán Cortés	Spanish conquistador who conquered the Aztecs in A.D. 1521 after arriving on the coast of Vera Cruz in A.D. 1519.
Malinche	Cortés's native female translator who is considered a traitor in Mexico today.
Cuauhtemoc	The last king of the Aztec who surrendered to Cortés in A.D. 1521 after an 85-day siege of the city.

14: SOUTH AMERICA

14.1 EARLY SOUTH AMERICA

Similar to North America and Mesoamerica, South America was occupied by humans during the Pleistocene epoch. Beginning with the Holocene epoch, at around 10,000 years ago, people took advantage of warmer climates and a variety of ecological zones to hunt, gather, and fish, and exploit a variety of plant resources. The site of El Paraiso, located in coastal Peru, has been excavated and contained evidence of early Holocene subsistence activities. Material from the site suggests the region was occupied around 9,000 years ago and people subsisted mainly on fish and shellfish from the coast and also hunted deer and small mammals and gathered plants from the interior. Around 5,000 years ago, the site became a permanent settlement with nine stone structures that had several rooms and the walls were made of stone and painted red, black, and white (Moseley, 1975). In addition to fishing, the people subsisted on domesticated plants, such as gourds, squash, beans, and chili peppers, and also grew cotton for clothing and fishnets.

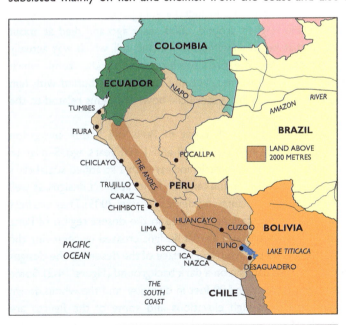

Figure 14-1. Map of western South America showing some prehistoric sites.

Another early complex site in Peru is Chavín de Huántar, which is located in the Andean Highlands and was occupied around 3,000 years ago. Architecture at the site includes stone platforms, a main plaza, a circular plaza, and temples. The circular plaza is 66 feet across and has a carved stone floor and walls of granite. The largest temple is Castillo, which was over 45 feet high, contained many relief sculptures and had a large sculpture (known as the Lanzon) that depicts a fanged deity (Chazan, 2011). Another temple was U-shaped and had bas-relief carvings along the wall of jaguars, caimans, and humans. The Chavín culture influenced an area that extended throughout northern and central Peru. The artistic style of jaguars, snakes, caimans, humans, and geometric designs are found through the highlands and coast. Also, the Chavín people began to rely more heavily on domesticated plants and included potatoes and quinoa to their subsistence base. They also domesticated llamas as beasts of burden, and for wool and meat.

14.2 PREDECESSORS OF THE INCA

Around 2,000 years ago, the Moche Culture evolved along the northern Peruvian coast (Chazan, 2011). This culture is best known for its architecturally impressive sites, descriptive art, elaborate pottery, and metallurgy. The Moche social structure was stratified with leaders, priests and warriors living in the city centers. Middle class individuals, such as artists and merchants lived in the outskirts of the cities, and farmers and fishermen lived in the rural areas. Some of the most elaborate Moche ceramics are human head effigy vessels, painted vessels showing warriors, and animal effigy vessels. Moche art often depicts ceremonies, some of which involve human sacrifice, warfare, and deities. Their metal work used gold, silver, and copper to make jewelry for the elite and for religious offerings.

The largest site of the Moche Culture is the site of Sipan, in northern Peru. At this site, the burial of the Lord of Sipan illustrates the power of the elite and the complexity of burial rituals among the Moche. The Lord of Sipan was buried with six other people, including three women (possibly wives or concubines), two servants, and a child (Scarre, 2005). In addition to the human remains, a dog skeleton was also found. The Lord of Sipan was buried in beautifully made cotton textiles, and his burial offerings included a gold pectoral, gold and silver necklace, nose rings, earrings, a helmet, and bracelets. He reigned around 1,800 years ago and died at about 40 years of age. Examination of his remains indicated that he was five feet five inches tall, which was actually quite tall for that time period (Durrani, 2009). Excavation below the lord's tomb revealed another tomb, which may have been of a priest, because the artifacts buried with him were religious, including a sacrificial bowl and items related to the worship of the moon.

Located on the south coast of Peru, the Nazca civilization reached its height between 1,800 and 1,400 years ago. Similar to the Moche, it was a militaristic society with a stratified social class structure. Their pottery and textiles depict abstract designs, as well as animals, humans, plants, and deities (Scarre, 2005). They are best known for the Nazca Lines, located in the desert region of Peru. These are geometric and animal designs created by removing the darker rocks and soil from the surface of the desert so the designs appear as a light pattern on a dark background (Figure 14-2). Some of the figures are over 500 feet in diameter and the whole design is best seen from high elevations and some of the figures are hundreds of feet in diameter. There are many theories regarding their purpose. One explanation is that the line drawings may have been formed for the gods and were related to the Nazca worship

Figure 14-2. The "Monkey," a Nazca line drawing.

of water deities (Reinhard, 1996). In another hypothesis, the lines were created as an astronomical observatory. Whatever their purpose, the time and effort needed to create them indicates their significance to the Nazca people.

Another Civilization, called the Tiwanaku, dominated the south central Andes region between 1,600 and 1,000 years ago. The capital city (also called Tiwanaku) covered approximately two square miles and had a population of around 15,000–30,000 people (Kolata, 1993). The city is best known for its stone architecture, which used cut stone blocks that came from a quarry six miles away and some of the largest stones weighed over 140 tons. The site also had a drainage system to divert waste from the city and also to collect fresh rainwater for drinking and irrigation. One area of the site is a cross-shaped pyramid that is over 52 feet tall. A platform near the pyramid was made of soil faced with stone blocks. Another area of the site was probably a ceremonial center and was decorated with yellow and red clay. The most prominent structure at Tiwanaku is the Gateway of the Sun, located in a courtyard to the north of the site. This gate has a lintel that depicts winged deities carved in bas-relief (Scarre, 2005).

Contemporary with Tiwanaku was the Wari civilization, located in northern Peru. They are believed to be very war-like and, as they expanded their territory through warfare, they also built road systems and terraced fields. The terraced fields increased agricultural production and the roads made trade and transportation easier. The capital city, also called Wari, covered six square miles and had a central area with religious and government structures, as well as residential areas. Archaeological excavations of the site indicate that the buildings were coated with white plaster and may also have been painted. At around 1,000 years ago, both the Tiwanaku and Wari civilizations collapsed, which may be due to drier climates brought about by climate change (Scarre, 2005) and political destabilization related to the lack of food.

The Chimú civilization almost certainly grew out of the Moche Culture in northern Peru and eventually came to dominate much of Peru by 700 years ago. The Chimú's economy was centered on trade, particularly ceramics, metallurgy, and textiles. The ceramics were used for both domestic and ceremonial activities; and the ceremonial vessels and statues depicted a variety of motifs, such as animals, humans, and deities. Metal work used gold, silver, and copper for jewelry and other artifacts. Items were made for both trade and religious rituals. Textiles were made from alpaca wool (alpacas are a domestic animal similar to llamas) and dyed before being woven into elaborate designs. This economy was controlled by the elite in the capital of Chan Chan. Chan Chan covered an area of about ten square miles and may have been home to as many as 50,000 people. The city is composed of ten walled areas that contained ceremonial areas, tombs and temples, and residences. The walls were made from mud brick and covered with a plaster surface in which designs were carved (Scarre, 2005). Some of the walls at Chan Chan were originally 50 feet high and the carvings on the walls depict animals, people, and abstract designs. The Chimú were conquered by the Inca around A.D. 1470.

14.3 INCA EMPIRE

The Inca were a Quechua-speaking group that originated in the highlands of the Andes near Lake Titicaca. They expanded their territory by warfare (as was the case with the Wari), but also by diplomatic negotiations (Mosely, 2001). Their political structure was very stratified. At the top of the structure was the "Inca," who was the ruler, and his family. The nobility practiced cranial deformation (deliberately deforming the shape of children's skulls as they grow by tightly binding them with cloth), which gave an obvious visual indication of their status. Following the nobility in status were the priests and then military commanders. The capital of the Inca was

Figure 14-3. A View of Machu Picchu, Peru (Image by Charles J. Sharp).

at Cuzco and the vast empire (which covered Peru and parts of Ecuador and Chile) was also governed by regional commanders. Government was aided by a road system and a recording system called a quipu. They also standardized measurements and a calendar system to make trade and communication easier throughout the empire.

Although much of the Incan capital of Cuzco has been covered over by modern architecture, some of the original structures remain. The Spanish recorded that the capital was laid out in the shape of a mountain lion, with the river serving as the spine, the ceremonial center (known as Sacsayhuaman) as the head, and the main city center as the body. The Inca used a unique trapezoidal shape for their carved stones that made up the city structures. This construction can be seen in the ceremonial center, or Sacsayhuaman, which consists of a large plaza, several large structures, and storage rooms. The ceremonial area also had at least three large stone walls that were six feet tall and over one thousand feet long.

Another important Incan site is the city of Machu Picchu, which was built around A.D. 1450 (Figure 14-3). The city was not discovered until 1911 by archaeologist Hiram Bingham. It was probably built by either Pachacuti Inca or Tupac Inca (Inca rulers) and was divided into three sections, including a ceremonial center, an elite residential area, and a commoner residential area. Made of similar construction to Cuzco, the ceremonial center contains the famous Temple of the Sun, the Intihuatana stone, and the Room of the Three Windows. The Temple of the Sun was built so that when the sun comes through the window of the temple on the winter solstice, it lights up a large ceremonial stone. Another large stone is the Intihuatana stone, which is arranged to point directly at the sun during the winter solstice. The Room of the Three Windows is located near the main temple and the Intihuatana stone. These structures have been used by some scholars to suggest that Machu Picchu was strictly a ceremonial site (Reinhard, 2007). Others argue that it was a royal estate for the Pachacuti Inca (Burger and Salazar, 2004).

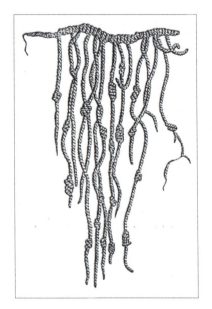

Figure 14-4. An Incan quipu.

The Inca civilization has many similarities with the Aztec civilization discussed in Chapter 13. Both had powerful rulers with a strict hierarchy, elaborate ceremony and ritual, human sacrifice, monumental architecture, trade networks, and high agricultural production. However, the Incan empire did not have a written language system. They did have a means of keeping track of trade and tribute with a quipu (also called a khipu), which was made out of cotton or wool and had a main, woven cord with pendant cords (Figure 14-4). The pendant cords were knotted as a recording system to document population numbers, inventories, tribute records, and other transactions. Simple knots, long knots, and figure-eight knots were positioned on the cords to record numbers (Ascher and Ascher, 1978).

The empire was controlled by an elaborate system of "roads," known as the Inca Trail, these roads varied from pathways to wide, paved corridors. Some bridges connecting the roads were actually carved out of cliff faces in some of the more mountainous areas of the empire. The roads were manned by runners who lived in huts along the trail and were ready to transmit messages to the furthest areas of the empire. For example, a message relating to warfare or other important government issues could be sent from Cuzco and passed along by the runners to the border areas. Considering that the Inca Empire spanned thousands of miles, this was truly an important innovation.

The Inca had many deities, but one of the most important was the sun god. They also believed in reincarnation and buried their dead in tombs and burial pits, but never cremated their dead because they believed they would not be reincarnated if that occurred. The Inca practiced two forms of human sacrifice; one type was with the sacrificing of people to be buried with the rulers upon their death and the other was sacrificing children in the mountain regions of the Andes. These child sacrifices were known as capacocha and the remains that have been found were frequently naturally mummified due to the cold dry temperatures on the high mountain peaks (Reinhard and Ceruti, 2010). The children were buried wearing finely made clothing and offerings such as silver llama pins. Spanish records indicate that the children were chosen for their beauty and innocence. The mummified remains are extremely well preserved, with the skin, hair, and nails intact.

The end of the Incan Empire occurred with the arrival of the Spanish in A.D. 1532, led by Francisco Pizarro (Evans, 2008). The Spanish arrived at a time of upheaval in the Inca Empire, because it followed a civil war between half-brothers Huayna Capac and Atahualpa. The dispute arose when their father died and Huayna Capac became ruler. Atahualpa was a great warrior with the power of the armies behind him, so he launched a war against his brother to take the thrown. Atahualpa won the civil war, but when he met with the Spanish, they took him captive (Somervill, 2005). Under arrest, Atahualpa ruled for eight months from a prison compound in Cuzco. Pizarro ransomed Atahualpa and demanded that a room be filled once with gold and twice with silver. All over the empire, gold and silver objects and raw ore were sent to the capital. Atahualpa's ransom, which was recorded by the Spanish, was worth almost 250 million dollars in today's market. Unfortunately, instead of freeing Atahualpa, Pizarro had him tried for treason and he was found guilty. The penalty for treason was to be burned at the stake, but, as previously mentioned, the Inca buried their bodies whole for reincarnation. So, Atahualpa converted to Christianity and instead was strangled. It is a regrettable ending for such a vast empire, but it is important to remember that the descendants of the Inca still celebrate some of the ancient traditions and speak the Quechua language.

14.4 BRINGING IT TOGETHER

South America was colonized by humans at the end of the last Ice Age who lived for many thousands of years as hunters, gatherers, and fisher people. Eventually, people began to intensively cultivate plants and domesticate animals, such as llamas. Villages, such as El Paraiso and Chavín de Huántar, are testaments to increasing social complexity in western South America. Around 2,000 years ago, cultures such as the Moche evolved with innovations in ceramics, metallurgy, and irrigation. There was also clear social stratification and the elite were buried with human sacrifices and elaborate grave goods, as was the case with the Lord of Sipan. The Nazca are another culture that began to produce ceramics and gold, silver, and copper artifacts. However, the Nazca are best known for their large line drawings in the desert regions. These figures are created on the desert floor by removing rocks and dirt and depict animals, humans, and abstract figures. Following the Moche and Nazca cultures, the Tiwanaku civilization came to dominate the south central Andes region around 1,600 years ago. The capital city of Tiwanaku covered approximately two square miles and had a population of around 15,000–30,000 people with monumental structures, tombs, and residential areas. During that same time, the Wari culture arose in the north of Peru and was characterized by a large regional center, terraced agricultural fields, and a road system. Around 1,000 years ago, both the Tiwanaku and Wari civilizations collapsed. In northern Peru, the Chimú civilization came to dominate the area by around 700 years ago. Economy of the Chimú society was centered on trade and manufacture, particularly of ceramics, metallurgy, and textiles. The capital of Chimú was a city called Chan Chan, which covered an area of about ten square miles and housed 50,000 people. Despite the size of the Chimú civilization and the sociopolitical organization at Chan Chan, the Chimú were defeated by the Inca in A.D. 1470. The Inca civilization arose in the Andes region of Peru and quickly expanded its empire through warfare and diplomatic acquisition. It controlled its empire from Cuzco through an extensive road system, regional governors and a recording system called a quipu. The great city of Machu Picchu was built in the remote highlands as either a ceremonial site or a king's estate and was not discovered until A.D. 1911. The Spanish arrived in the region around A.D. 1535 during a time of civil unrest and the ruler Atahualpa was taken captive by the conquistador Pizarro and held for ransom. Although the ransom was paid, Atahualpa was found guilty of treason and executed, and the region became controlled by the Spanish.

Key Terms and Concepts

El Paraiso	A site occupied 9,000 years ago, evidence suggests that people subsisted on fish and shellfish, deer and small mammals, and plants.
Chavín de Huántar	A site located in the Andean Highlands and was occupied around 3,000 years ago and has evidence of early public architecture and domestic plants and animals.
Moche	A culture that evolved along the coast in northern Peru around 2,000 years ago and built architecturally impressive sites, made decorative pottery, and created ornamental objects out of gold, silver, and copper.
Lord of Sipan	A Moche burial of a ruler with human sacrifices and elaborate grave goods.
Nazca	A culture located on the south coast of Peru that reached its height between 1,800 and 1,400 years ago.
Nazca lines	Large geometric, animal, and human figures drawn in the desert region of southern Peru by the Nazca.
Tiwanaku	A civilization that dominated the south-central Andes region between 1,600 and 1,000 years ago.
Tiwanaku city	The capital of the Tiwanaku civilization that covered approximately two square miles and had a population of around 15,000–30,000 people.
Wari	A civilization contemporary with Tiwanaku, located in northern Peru; the capital city is also called Wari.

Chimú	A civilization that probably grew out of the Moche culture in northern Peru and eventually came to dominate much of Peru by 700 years ago.
Chan Chan	Capital city of the Chimú civilization that covered an area of about ten square miles and housed 50,000 people.
Inca	A Quechua-speaking group that originated in the highlands of the Andes near Lake Titicaca. Their empire eventually covered most of Peru, Ecuador, and Chile.
Cuzco	The capital of the Inca with monuments and buildings constructed of precisely fitted trapezoidal stone blocks.
Machu Picchu	A city in the Andes Highlands the was not discovered until the early 20th century by Bingham. May have been either a ceremonial site or a royal estate.
The Temple of the Sun	Was built so that when the sun comes through the window of the temple on the winter solstice, it lights up a ceremonial stone.
Intihuatana stone	Arranged to point directly at the sun during the winter solstice.
Quipu	A means of keeping track of trade and tribute with a quipu by using cotton cords tied with knots to represent counts of items.
Capacocha	Child sacrifices of the Inca in the Andes Highlands; they were frequently naturally mummified due to the cold dry temperatures.
Francisco Pizarro	Conquistador who led the conquest of the Inca.
Atahualpa	The last ruler of the Inca.

REFERENCES CITED

Adovasio, J. M., Donahue, J., Stuckenrath, R. (1990). The Meadowcroft Rockshelter Radiocarbon Chronology 1975-1990. *American Antiquity*, 55(2), 348-354.

Andrews, C. (1985). *The British Museum Book of the Rosetta Stone*. London: Dorset Press.

Argent, G. (2010). Do the clothes make the horse? Relationality, Roles and Satuses in Iron Age Inner Asia. *World Archaeology*, 42: 2, 157-174.

Ascher, M., Ascher, R. (1978). *Code of the Quipu: Databook*. Ann Arbor, MI: University of Michigan Press.

Asfaw, B., White, T., Lovejoy, C. O., Latimer, B., Simpson, S., Suwa, G. (1999). *Australopithecus garhi*: A New Species of Early Hominid from Ethiopia. *Science* 284 (5414), 629–35.

Bahn, P. G. (2007). *Cave Art*. London: Frances Lincoln.

Balistier, T. (2000). *The Phaistos Disc: An Account of its Unsolved Mystery*. Oakville, CT: David Brown Books.

Balter, V., Bocherens, H., Person, A., Labourdette, N., Renard M., Vandermeersch, B. (2002). Ecological and physiological variability of Sr/Ca and Ba/Ca in mammals of West European mid-Würmian food webs. *Palaeogeography, Palaeoclimatology, Palaeoecology*. 186 (1-2), 127–143.

Blench, R. M., McDonald, K. C., eds. (2000). *The Origins and Development of African Livestock: Archaeology, Genetics, Lingustics, and Ethnograpy*. London: University College London Press.

Bonfante, Larissa (1990). *Etruscan*. Berkeley and Los Angeles, CA: University of California Press.

Bortenschlager, S., Oeggl, K., (Eds.). (2000). *The Iceman and His Natural Environment: Palaeobotanical Results*. New York, N.Y.: Springer.

Broodbank, C., Strasser, T. F. (1991). Migrant farmers and the Neolithic Colonization of Crete. *Antiquity* 65(247), 233–245.

Brunet, M., Guy, F., Pilbeam, D., Mackaye, H. T., Likius, A., Ahounta, D., ... Zollikofer, C.. (2002). A new hominid from the Upper Miocene of Chad, Central Africa. *Nature*. 418, 145-151.

Burger, R., Salazar, L. (eds.) (2004). *Machu Picchu: Unveiling the Mystery of the Incas*. New Haven, CT: Yale University Press.

Capasso, L., Michetti, E., D'Anastasio, R. (2008). A Homo erectus hyoid bone: possible implications for the origin of the human capability for speech. *Collegium Antropologicum*. 32(4), 1007-1011.

Callender, G. (2000). The Middle Kingdom Renaissance. In, I. Shaw (Ed.), *The Oxford History of Ancient Egypt*. Oxford: Oxford University Press.

Castleden, R. (2005). *The Mycenaeans*. New York, NY: Routledge Press.

Castleden, R. (1990). *The Knossos Labyrinth: A New View of the 'Palace of Minos' at Knossos*. New York, NY: Routledge Press.

Chatters, J. C. (2002). *Ancient Encounters: Kennewick Man & the First Americans*. New York, NY: Simon & Schuster.

Chang, K. (1986). *The Archaeology of Ancient China*. New Haven, CT: Yale University Press.

Chazan, M. (2011). *World Prehistory and Archaeology* (2nd ed). Upper Saddle River, NJ: Prentice Hall.

Clark, G. (1954). *Excavations at Star Carr: an early Mesolithic site at Seamer near Scarborough, Yorkshire*. Cambridge, UK: Cambridge University Press.

Coe, M. D. (1992). *Breaking the Maya Code*. London: Thames & Hudson.

Coe, M. D. (1999). *The Maya*. (6th ed.). London and New York: Thames & Hudson.

Conneller, C. (2007). Inhabiting new landscapes: settlement and mobility in Britain after the last glacial maximum. *Oxford Journal of Archaeology*, 26(3), 1468-0092.

Crawford, H. (1993). *Sumer and the Sumerians*. New York, NY: Cambridge University Press.

Daniels, D. J., ed. (2004) *Ground Penetrating Radar* (2nd ed.). London: Institution of Engineering and Technology.

Dart, R. (1925) *Australopithecus africanus,* The man-ape of South Africa. *Nature*. 115, 195-199.

Dawson, R. (1982). *Confucius*. Oxford: Oxford University Press.

Diamond, J. (1999). *Guns, Germs and Steel*. New York, NY: W.W. Norton & Company, Inc.

Diaz del Castillo, B. (1956). *The Discovery and Conquest of Mexico*. New York, NY: Farrar, Straus, and Cudahy.

Dillehay, T. D. (1989). *Monte Verde: A Late Pleistocene Settlement in Chile*. Washington, DC: Smithsonian Institution Press.

Driver, G. R., Miles, J. C. (2007). *The Babylonian Laws*. Eugene, OR: Wipf and Stock.

Durband, A. C. (2008). Artificial cranial deformation in Pleistocene Australians: the Coobool Creek sample. *Journal of Human Evolution*. 54(6),795-813.

Durrani, N. (2009). Tombs of the Lord of Sipan. *World Archaeology*. Retrieved from http://www.world-archaeology.com/features/tombs-of-the-lords-of-sipan/.

Ebrey, P. B. (1999). *The Cambridge Illustrated History of China*. Cambridge: Cambridge University Press.

Unesco World Heritage Centre. (2012). Etruscan Necropolises of Cerveteri and Tarquinia. Retreived from http://whc.unesco.org/en/list/1158.

Evans, S. T. (2008). *Ancient Mexico and Central America: Archaeology and Culture History* (2nd ed.). London: Thames and Hudson.

Fagan, B. (2004). *The Long Summer: how climate changed civilization*. New York, NY: Basic Books.

Fagan, B. (2006). *People of the Earth*. (12th ed.). Upper Saddle River, NJ: Prentice Hall.

Fagan, B. (2009). *The Great Warming: Climate Change and the Rise and Fall of Civilizations*. New York, NY: Bloomsbury Press.

Fagles, R. (Trans.). (1991) *The Iliad*. New York, NY: Penguin Books.

Fairbank, J. K., Goldman, M. (2006). *China: A New History* (2nd ed.). Cambridge, MA: Harvard University Press.

Fenton, A. (1978). *Northern Isles: Orkney and Shetland*. Edinburgh, Scotland: John Donald Publishers Ltd.

Flannery, K. V. (1969). The origins and ecological effects of early domestication in Iran and the Near East. In A. B. Damania, J. Valkoun, G. Willcox, C. O. Qualset (Eds.), *The Domestication and Exploitation of Plants and Animals*. Chicago: Aldine.

Flannery, K. V. (1976). *The Early Mesoamerican Village*. Walnut Creek, CA: Left Coast Press.

Fowler, B. (2000). *Iceman: Uncovering the Life and Times of a Prehistoric Man Found in an Alpine Glacier*. New York, N.Y.: Random House.

Germonpréa, M., Sablin, M. V. (2008). Fossil dogs and wolves from Palaeolithic sites in Belgium, the Ukraine and Russia: osteometry, ancient DNA and stable isotopes. *Journal of Archaeological Science*. 36(2), 473-490.

Gernet, J. (1996). *A History of Chinese Civilization* (2nd ed.). Cambridge: Cambridge University Press.

Gesell, G. C., Day, L. P., Coulson, W. D. E. (1995). Excavatons at Kavousi, Crete, 1989 and 1990. *Hesperia: The Journal of the American School of Classical Studies at Athens*. 64(1), 67-120.

Gibson, J. L. (2000). *The Ancient Mounds of Poverty Point: Place of Rings*. Gainesville, FL: University Press of Florida.

Goodall, J. (1969). *My Friends the Wild Chimpanzees* Washington, DC: National Geographic Society.

Goodall, J. (1986). *The Chimpanzees of Gombe: Patterns of Behavior*. Boston: Bellknap Press.

Green, R. E., Krause, J., Briggs, A. W., Maricic, T., Stenzel, U., Kircher, M., ...Paabo, S. (2010). A Draft Sequence of the Neanderthal Genome. *Science*. 328(5979), 710–722.

Groube, L., Chappell, J. M., Muke, J., Price, D. (1989). A 40,000 year-old human occupation site at Huon Peninsula, Papua New Guinea. *Nature*. 324, 453-455.

Habu, J. (2004). *Ancient Jomon of Japan*. Cambridge: Cambridge University Press.

Healy, M. (1991). *The Ancient Assyrians*. London: Osprey.

Hively, R., Horn, R. (2006). A Statistical Study of Lunar Alignments at the Newark Earthworks. *Midcontinental Journal of Archaeology*. Retrieved from HighBeam Research: http://www.highbeam.com/doc/1P3-1199602541.html.

Hodder, I. (2006). *The Leopard's Tale: Revealing the Mysteries of Çatalhöyük*. London:New York:Thames & Hudson.

Hollenbach, K. D. (2009). *Foraging in the Tennessee River Valley*. Tuscaloosa, AL: University of Alabama Press.

Howell, F. C. (1957). The Evolutionary Significance of Variation and Varieties of 'Neanderthal' Man. *The Quarterly Review of Biology*. 32(4), 330–347.

Hunt, Kevin D. (1996). The postural feeding hypothesis: An Ecological Model for the Evolution of Bipedalism. *South African Journal of Science*. 92, 77-90.

Janssens, P. A. (1970). *Paleopathology: Diseases and Injuries of Prehistoric Man*. USA: Atlantic Highlands, NJ: Humanities Press Inc.

Johanson, D. C., Maitland, A. E. (1981). *Lucy: The Beginning of Humankind*. New York, NY: Simon and Schuster.

Jordania, J. (2011). *Why do People Sing? Music in Human Evolution*. Berlin: Logos.

Kearey, P. (2001). *Dictionary of Geology* (2nd ed.). London: Penguin Reference.

Kenyon, K. M. (1957). *Digging up Jericho*. London: Ernest Benn.

Kirkland, R. (2004). *Taoism: The Enduring Tradition*. London and New York: Routledge.

Kolata, A. L. (1993). *The Tiwanaku: Portrait of an Andean Civilization*. Oxford: Wiley-Blackwell.

Kottak, C. (2011). *Cultural Anthropology: Appreciating Cultural Diversity*. New York, NY: McGraw Hill.

Kreis, S. (2002) *The History Guide*. Retrieved from Lecture notes online web site: http://www.historyguide.org/ancient/lecture3b.html.

Laing, L. (1974). *Orkney and Shetland: An Archaeological Guide*. Newton Abbott: David and Charles Ltd.

Leakey, M. D. (1981). Discoveries at Laetoli in Northern Tanzania. Proceedings of the Geologists' Association. 92 (2), 81–86

Leakey, M. G., Feibel, C. S., MacDougall, I., Walker, A. (1995). New four-million-year-old hominid species from Kanapoi and Allia Bay, Kenya. *Nature* 376 (6541), 565–571.

Leakey, L.S.B., Tobias, P.V., Napier, J.R. (1965). A New Species of Genus *Homo* from Olduvai Gorge. *Current Anthropology*. 6(4), 7-9.

Leick, G. (2003). *Mesopotamia*. New York, NY: Penguin Press.

Legg, A. J., Rowley-Conwy, P. A. (1988) *Star Carr revisited*. University of London, London: Centre for Extra-Mural Studies.

Lewis, M. E. (2007). *The Early Chinese Empires: Qin and Han*. London: Belknap Press.

Li, X. (2002). The Xia-Shang-Zhou Chronology Project: Methodology and results. *Journal of East Asian Archaeology*. 4(1-4), 321–333.

Lieberman, P. (2007) The Evolution of Human Speech: Its Anatomical and Neural Bases. *Current Anthropology*. 48(1), 39-66.

Lehner, M. (1997). *The Complete Pyramids*. London: Thames and Hudson.

Liverani, M., Bahrani, Z., Van de Mieroop, M. (2006). *Uruk: The First City*. London: Equinox Publishing.

Lovejoy, C. O. (1981). The Origin of Man. *Science*. 211(4480), 341-50.

Marinatos, N. (1993). *Minoan Religion: Ritual, Image, and Symbol*. Columbia, SC: University of South Carolina Press.

Martin, P. S. (1989). Prehistoric overkill: A global model. In P. S. Martin, R. G. Klein (Eds.), *Quaternary extinctions: A prehistoric revolution*. Tucson, AZ: Univ. Arizona Press

Mausoleum of the First Qin Emperor. (2012). Retrieved from http://whc.unesco.org/pg.cfm?cid=31&id_site=441.

McEnroe, J. C. (2010). *Architecture of Minoan Crete: constructing identity in the Aegean Bronze Age*. Austin, TX: University of Texas Press.

Mitchell, S. (2004). *Gilgamesh: A New English Version*. New York: Free Press.

Molleson, T. (1994). The Eloquent Bones of Abu Hureyra. *Scientific American*. 271(2), 70–75.

Moore, A. M. T., Hillman, G.C., Legge, A. J. (2001). *Village on the Euphrates*. Oxford: Oxford University Press.

Morey, D. F. (2010). *Dogs: Domestication and the Development of a Social Bond*. New York, NY: Cambridge University Press.

Morey, D. F., Wiant, M. D. (1992). Early Holocene Domestic Dog Burials from the North American Midwest. *Current Anthropology*. 33(2), 224-229.

Moseley, M. E. (1975). *The Maritime foundations of Andean Civilization*. Menlo Park, CA: Cummings Publishing Company.

Moseley, M. E. (2001). *The Incas and their Ancestors* (Revised 2nd ed.). London: Thames & Hudson.

Moulherat, C., M., Tengberg, J. F., Haquet, M. B. (2002). First evidence of cotton at Neolithic Mehrgarh, Pakistan: Analysis of mineralized fibres from a copper bead. *Journal of Archaeological Science*. 29(12), 1393–1401.

Needham, J. (1972). *Science and Civilization in China: Volume 1, Introductory Orientations*. London: Syndics of the Cambridge University Pres.

Nerlich, A. G., Peschel, O., Egarter-Vigl, E. (2009). New evidence for Ötzi's final trauma *Intensive Care Medicine*. 35(6), 1138-1139.

Neusius, S.W., Gross, G.T. (2007). *Seeking Our Past: An Introduction to North American Archaeology*. New York, Oxford: Oxford University Press.

O'Connell, J. F., Allen, J. (2004). Dating the colonization of Sahul (Pleistocene Australia--New Guinea): A review of recent research. *Journal of Archaeological Science*. 31, 835-853.

Ovodov, N. D., Crockford, S. J., Kuzmin, Y.V., Higham, T. F. G., Hodgins, G. W. L. (2011). A 33,000-Year-Old Incipient Dog from the Altai Mountains of Siberia: Evidence of the Earliest Domestication Disrupted by the Last Glacial Maximum. *PLoS ONE*. 6(7), e22821.

Owsley D.W., Jantz R. L. (2001). Archaeological politics and public interest in paleoamerican studies: lessons from Gordon Creek Woman and Kennewick Man. *American Antiquity*. 66(4), 565-575.

Pauketat, T. R. (2004). *Ancient Cahokia and the Mississippians*. Cambridge, MA: Cambridge University Press.

Pauketat, T. R. (2009). *Cahokia: Ancient America's Great City on the Mississippi*. New York, NY: The Viking Press.

Pike, A. W. G., Hoffmann, D. L., García-Diez, M., Pettitt, P. B., Alcolea, J., De Balbín, R., González-Sainz, C., de las Heras, C., Lasheras, J.A., Montes, R., Zilhão, J. (2012). U-Series Dating of Paleolithic Art in 11 Caves in Spain. *Science*. 336(6087), 1409-1413.

Pollard, J. (2008). *Prehistoric Britain*. Oxford, England: Blackwell Publishing Ltd.

Prufer, K., Munch, K., Hellmann, I., Akagi, K., Miller, J., Walenz, B., …Eichler, E. E. (2012). The Bonobo Genome Compared with the Chimpanzee and Human Genomes. *Nature*. Retrieved from http://www.nature.com/nature/journal/vaop/ncurrent/full/nature11128.html.

Reinhard, J. (1996). *The Nazca Lines: A New Perspective on their Origin and Meaning* (6th ed.). Lima: Los Pinos.

Reinhard, J. (2007). *Machu Picchu: Exploring an Ancient Sacred Center*. Los Angeles, CA: Cotsen Institute of Archaeology.

Reinhard, J., Ceruti, C. (2010). *Inca Rituals and Sacred Mountains: A Study of the World's Highest Archaeological Sites*. Los Angeles, CA: Cotsen Institute of Archaeology.

Relethford, J. H. (2009). *The Human Species: An Introduction to Biological Anthropology* (8th ed.). New York, NY: McGraw Hill.

Restall, M. (2003). *Seven Myths of the Spanish Conquest*. Oxford: Oxford University Press.

Richards, M. P., Pettitt, P. B., Trinkaus, E., Smith, F. H., Paunović, M., Karavanić, I. (2000). Neanderthal diet at Vindija and Neanderthal predation: The evidence from stable isotopes. *Proceedings of the National Academy of Sciences U S A*. 97(13), 7663–7666.

Rigaud, J-P., Simek, J. F., Thierry, G. E. (1995). Mousterian fires from Grotte XVI (Dordogne, France). *Antiquity*. 69, 902-912.

Roberts, C., Manchester, K. (1995). *The Archaeology of Disease*. Cornell, NY: Cornell University Press.

Roberts, M. (2010). "Malaria and weak bones' may have killed Tutankhamun. Retrieved from http://news.bbc.co.uk/2/hi/health/8516425.stm.

Robertson, G. B., Prescott, J. R. (2006). Luminescence dating at the archaeological and human burial site at Roonka, South Australia. *Quaternary Science Reviews*. 25(19–20), 2586–2593.

Ryan, K. (2005). The Origins of Pastoralism in Eastern Africa. *Expedition*. 47(3), 43-45.

Scarre, C. (2005). *The Human Past: World Prehistory and the Development of Human Societies*. London: Thames and Hudson.

Schiff, S. (2011). *Cleopatra: A Life*. Lebanon, IN: Back Bay Books.

Scott, K. (1986). The Large Mammal Fauna. In P. Callow and J. M. Cornford (Eds.), *La Cotte de St. Brelade 1961-1978*, 109-138. Norwich, UK: Geo Books.

Senut, B., Pickford, M., Gommery, D., Mein, P., Cheboi, K., Coppens, Y. (2001) First hominid from the Miocene (Lukeino Formation, Kenya). *Comptes Rendus de l'Academie de Sciences*. 332(2), 137-144.

Seeher, J. (1999). *Ma'adi and Wadi Digla*. In, Encyclopedia of the Archaeology of Ancient Egypt. London: Psychology Press.

Sherwood, S. C., Driskell, B. N., Randall, A. R., Meeks, S. C. (2004). Chronology and Stratigraphy at Dust Cave, Alabama. *American Antiquity*. 69(3), 533-554.

Singh, U. (2008). *A history of ancient and early medieval India: from the Stone Age to the 12th century*. New Delhi, Upper Saddle River, NJ: Pearson Education.

Smuts, J. (1973) *Holism and Evolution*. Westport, CT: Greenwood Publishing.

Solecki, R. S. (1975). Shanidar IV, a Neanderthal Flower Burial in Northern Iraq". *Science* 190(4217), 880–881.

Somervill, B. (2005). *Francisco Pizarro: Conqueror of the Incas*. North Mankato, MN: Compass Point Books.

Sorensen, B. (2009). Energy Use by Eem Neanderthals. *Journal of Archaeological Science*. 36(10), 2201–2205.

Stanford, D., Bradley, B. (2004). The North Atlantic ice-edge corridor: a possible Palaeolithic route to the New World. *World Archaeology*. 36(4), 459–478.

Stewart, T. D. (1977). The Neanderthal Skeletal Remains from Shanidar Cave, Iraq: A Summary of Findings to Date. *Proceedings of the American Philosophical Society*. 121(2), 121-165.

Star Carr Archaeology Project (2012). Retrieved from www.starcarr.com.

Struever, S., Holton, F. A. (2000) *Koster: Americans in Search of Their Prehistoric Past*. Long Grove, IL: Waveland Press.

Sukumar, R. (2003). *The Living Elephants: Evolutionary Ecology, Behaviour, and Conservation*. Oxford: Oxford University Press.

Svoboda, J. A. (2008). The Upper Paleolithic burial area at Predmostí: Ritual and Taphonomy. *Journal of Human Evolution.* 54(1), 15-33

Taylor, J. (2001). *Death and the Afterlife in Ancient Egypt.* Chicago: University of Chicago Press.

Trinkaus, E. (1985). Pathology and posture of the La Chapelle-aux-Saints Neanderthal. *American Journal of Physical Anthropology* 67(1), 19-41.

Turner, C. G., Turner, J. A. (1992). The First Claim for Cannibalism in the Southwest: Walter Hough's 1901 Discovery at Canyon Butte Ruin 3, Northeastern Arizona. *American Antiquity.* 57(4), 661-682.

Tyldesley, J. (2000). *Ramesses: Egypt's Greatest Pharaoh.* London: Viking/Penguin Books.

Tylor, E. B. (1871). *Primitive Cultures.* New York, NY: Harper Row.

Van Noten, F., Polosmak, N. (1995). The Frozen Tomb of the Scythians. *Endeavour.* 19(2), 76-83.

Verner, M. (2001). *The Pyramids: The Mystery, Culture, and Science of Egypt's Great Monuments.* New York: Grove Press.

Vila, C., Savolainen, P., Maldonado, J. E., Rice, J. E., Honeycutt, R. L. (1997). Multiple and ancient origins of the domestic dog. *Science.* 276(5319), 1687.

Waldorf, D. C. (1994) *The Art of Flint Knapping. Fourth Edition.* Branson, MO: Mound Builder Books.

Walker, R. B. (1998). *Late Paleoindian through Middle Archaic Faunal Evidence from Dust Cave, Alabama.* PhD Dissertation. Knoxville, TN: University of Tennessee.

Walker, R. B., Morey, D. F., Relethford, J. H. (2005). Early and Mid-Holocene Dogs in Southeastern North America: Examples from Dust Cave. *Southeastern Archaeology* 24(1): 83-92.

Walker, R. B., Windham, R. J. (n.d.). The Dogs of Spirit Hill, An Analysis of Domestic Dog Burials from Jackson County, Alabama. In T. Peres (Ed.), *Current Trends in Southeastern Zooarchaeology.* Gainesville, FL: University Press of Florida.

Webb, W. S. (1946). Indian Knoll, Site Oh2, Ohio County, Kentucky. *Univeristy of Kentucky, Reports in Anthropology and Archaeology.* 6, 113-365.

Wenke, R. (1991). The Evolution of Early Egyptian Civilization: Issues and Evidence, *Journal of World Prehistory.* 5(3), 279-329.

Wheeler, P. E. (1984). The Evolution of ipedality and Loss of Functional Body Hair in Hominids. *Journal of Human Evolution.* 13, 91-98.

White, T. D., Asfaw, B., Beyene, Y., Haile-Selassie, Y., Lovejoy, C. O., Suwa, G., WoldeGabriel, G. (2009). *Ardipithecus ramidus* and the Paleobiology of Early Hominids. *Science.* 326(5949), 75-86.

Whittaker, J. C. (1994) *Flintknapping: Making and Understanding Stone Tools.* Austin, TX: University of Texas Press.

Wolpoff, M. H., Hawks, J., Frayer, D. W., Hunley, K. (2001). Modern Human Ancestry at the Peripheries: A Test of the Replacement Theory. *Science.* 291(5502), 293-297.

Woolley, L. (1927). *Ur Excavations V: The Ziggurat and Its Surroundings.* Cambridge: Oxford University Press.

Woolley, L. (1939). *The Ziggurat and its Surroundings.* Ur Excavations, 5.

World's First Zoo - Hierakonpolis, Egypt. *Archaeology Magazine.* Retrieved from http://www.archaeology.org/1001/topten/egypt.html

Wright, D. C. (2001). *The History of China.* Westport, CT: Greenwood Publishing Group.

Zilhão, J., Trinkaus, E. (Eds.). (2002). *Portrait of the Artist as a Child. The Gravettian Human Skeleton from the Abrigo do Lagar Velho and its Archeological Context . Trabalhos de Arqueologia.* 22.

IMAGE CREDITS

Chapter 1

Figure 1-1. "Edward Burnett Tylor" © User:Beao / Wikimedia Commons / Public Domain.

Figure 1-2. Wikimedia Commons / Public Domain.

Figure 1-3. "Enseñando a Tallar" Copyright © 1987 by José-Manuel Benito Álvarez / Wikimedia Commons / CC BY-SA 2.5.

Chapter 2

Figure 2-2. "Skull of Sahelanthropus Tchadensis" Copyright © 2010 by Didier Descouens / Wikimedia Commons / CC BY-SA 3.0.

Figure 2-3. "Reconstruction of the Fossil Skeleton Lucy" Copyright © 2007 by User:Ephraim33 / Wikimedia Commons / CC BY-SA 3.0.

Figure 2-4. "Paranthropus Boisei Skull" Copyright © 2007 by User:Durova / Wikimedia Commons / CC BY-SA 3.0.

Figure 2-5. "Chopper" Copyright © 2010 by Didier Descouens / Wikimedia Commons / CC BY-SA 3.0.

Figure 2-6. "Turkana Boy" Copyright © 2008 by Claire Houck / Wikimedia Commons / CC BY-SA 2.0.

Figure 2-7. Victoria County History of Kent / Public Domain.

Chapter 3

Figure 3-2. "Homo Neanderthalensis" Copyright © 2011 by User: Anagoria / Wikimedia Commons / CC BY 3.0.

Figure 3-3. José-Manuel Benito / Wikimedia Commons / Public Domain.

Figure 3-4. José-Manuel Benito / Wikimedia Commons / Public Domain.

Figure 3-5. "Skhul V" Copyright © 2009 by User:Wapondaponda / Wikimedia Commons / CC BY-SA 3.0.

Figure 3-6. "Cro-Magnon Man Skull" Copyright © 2010 by User: Laténium / Wikimedia Commons / CC BY-SA 3.0.

Figure 3-7. U.S. National Park Service / Public Domain.

Figure 3-8. "Venus von Willendorf" Copyright © 2007 by MatthiasKabel / Wikimedia Commons / CC-BY 2.5.

Figure 3-9. User:HTO / Wikimedia Commons / Public Domain.

Figure 3-10. "Lascaux Caves" Copyright © 2005 by User:Peter80 / Wikimedia Commons / CC BY-SA 3.0.

Chapter 4

Figure 4-1. "Map of Sunda and Sahul" Copyright © 2007 by Maximilian Dörrbecker / Wikimedia Commons / CC BY-SA 3.0.

Figure 4-2. "Peruvian Deformity" Copyright © 2012 by Didier Descouens / Wikimedia Commons / CC BY-SA 3.0.

Figure 4-3. "Yankee Hat Art" Copyright © 2005 by User:Martyman / Wikimedia Commons / CC BY-SA 3.0.

Figure 4-4. Virginia Deptartment of Historic Resources / Public Domain.

Figure 4-5. User:Calame / Wikimedia Commons / Public Domain.

Figure 4-6. Charles R. Knight / Wikimedia Commons / Public Domain.

Chapter 5

Figure 5-1. User:Titleist46 / Wikimedia Commons / Public Domain.

Figure 5-2. Copyright © 2007 by User:Tyke / Wikimedia Commons / CC BY-SA 3.0.

Figure 5-4. Per Honor et Gloria / Wikimedia Commons / Public Domain.

Figure 5-5. Source: http://en.wikipedia.org/wiki/File:Mummy_of_the_Ukok_Princess.jpg. Copyright in the Public Domain.

Chapter 6

Figure 6-1. "Map of Fertile Crescent" Copyright © 2011 by User:Nafsadh / Wikimedia Commons / CC BY-SA 3.0.

Figure 6-2. Abraham Sobkowski / Wikimedia Commons / Public Domain.

Figure 6-3. "Model Room from Çatalhöyük" Copyright © 2007 by Georges Jansoone / Wikimedia Commons / CC BY-SA 3.0.

Figure 6-5. "Orkney Skara Brae" Copyright © 2002 by John F. Burka / Wikimedia Commons / CC BY-SA 3.0.

Chapter 7

Figure 7-2. "British Museum Room 10 Cuneiform" Copyright © 2011 by Matt Neale / British Museum (Assyrian Collections / CC BY 2.0.

Figure 7-3. User:Venerable Bede / Wikimedia Commons / Public Domain.

Figure 7-4. "Ancient Ziggurat at Ali Air Base Iraq" Copyright © 2005 by User:Hardnfast / Wikimedia Commons / CC BY 3.0.

Figure 7-5. Iraqi Directorate General of Antiquities / Wikimedia Commons / Public Domain.

Figure 7-6. Copyright © 2009 by User: Deror avi / Louvre Museum / Wikimedia Commons.

Figure 7-7. "Excavations of Tel Be'er Sheva" Copyright © 2007 by User:gugganij / Wikimedia Commons / CC BY-SA 3.0.

Figure 7-8. "The British Musuem, Room 6 - Assyrian Sculpture" Copyright © 2007 by Mujtaba Chohan / Wikimedia Commons / CC BY-SA 3.0.

Figure 7-9. "Palace Relief, Nimrud, Alabaster, 883-859 BC" Copyright © 2010 by Ealdgyth / Wikimedia Commons / CC BY-SA 3.0.

Chapter 8

Figure 8-2. "Rosetta Stone" Copyright © 2007 by Hans Hillewaert / Wikimedia Commons / CC BY-SA 3.0.

Figure 8-3. Jeff Dahl / Wikimedia Commons / Public Domain.

Figure 8-4. Jon Bodsworth / Egypt Archive / Public Domain.

Figure 8-5. Jon Bodsworth / Egypt Archive / Public Domain.

Chapter 9

Figure 9-2. "Throne Hall Knossos" Copyright © 2005 by User:Chris 73 / Wikimedia Commons / CC BY-SA 3.0.

Figure 9-3. User:ChrisO / Wikimedia Commons / Public Domain.

Figure 9-4. "Phaistos" Copyright © 2010 by User:Aserakov / Wikimedia Commons / CC BY-SA 3.0.

IMAGE CREDITS

Figure 9-5. "Snake Goddess from the Palace of Knossos" Copyright © 2005 by User:Chris 73 / Wikimedia Commons / CC BY-SA 3.0.

Figure 9-6. "The Lions Gate at Mycenae" Copyright © 2004 by David Monniaux / Wikimedia Commons / CC BY-SA 3.0.

Chapter 10

Figure 10-2. Per Honor et Gloria / Tokyo National Museum / Public Domain.

Figure 10-3. Source: http://en.wikipedia.org/wiki/File:Jiaguwen.jpg. Copyright in the Public Domain.

Figure 10-4. User:airunp / Wikimedia Commons / Public Domain.

Figure 10-5. "Terracotta Army" Copyright © 2006 by Tomasz Sienicki / Wikimedia Commons / CC BY 1.0.

Chapter 11

Figure 11-2. "Indus Valley Seals" Copyright © 2005 by World Imaging / Wikimedia Commons / CC BY-SA 3.0.

Figure 11-3. "Dancing Girl" Copyright © 2009 by User:Calliopejen1 / Wikimedia Commons / CC BY-SA 3.0.

Figure 11-4. "Mohenjo-daro" Copyright © 2006 by User:Grjatoi / Wikimedia Commons / CC BY-SA 3.0.

Chapter 12

Figure 12-1. "Mound at Poverty Point" Copyright © 2008 by User:kniemla / Flickr / CC BY-SA 2.0.

Figure 12-3. National Park Service / Public Domain.

Figure 12-4. "Monk's Mound, Cahokia" Copyright © 2011 by User:QuartierLatin1968 / Wikimedia Commons / CC BY-SA 3.0.

Figure 12-6. "Cliff Palace at Mesa Verde National Park" Copyright © 2007 by User:Staplegunther / Wikimedia Commons / CC BY 3.0.

Chapter 13

Figure 13-2. Bibi Saint-Pol / Wikimedia Commons / Public Domain.

Figure 13-3. User:Jackhynes / Wikimedia Commons / Public Domain.

Figure 13-4. "Tikal Temple" Copyright © 2006 by Raymond Ostertag / Wikimedia Commons / CC BY-SA 2.5.

Figure 13.5. User:ATSZ56 / Wikimedia Commons / Public Domain.

Figure 13-6. User:Thelmadatter / Wikimedia Commons / Public Domain.

Chapter 14

Figure 14-2. Maria Reiche / Wikimedia Commons / Public Domain.

Figure 14-3. "Machu Picchu" Copyright © 2012 by User:Charlesjsharp / Wikimedia Commons / CC BY-SA 3.0.

Figure 14-4. Wikimedia Commons / Public Domain.

INDEX

A

Absolute dating 12
Abu Hureyra 53
Acamapichtli 115
Acheulean hand axe 20
Adena 101, 106, 107
Ahmose I 72, 75
Ain Mallaha 52, 53, 58, 59
Akkadian Empire 63, 64, 66
Altamira Cave 30, 32
Amenhotep IV 72, 75
Amud 26
Amun 72, 73, 75
Anasazi 2, 104, 105, 106, 108
Ardipithecus ramidus 17, 21, 22
Artifacts 11, 12, 37, 70, 95, 103
Ashkelon 47
Ashoka 97, 98
Assyrian Empire 65, 66
Atahualpa 123, 124, 125
Aten 73, 75
Atlantic Crossing 38
Atlatl 28, 29
Aubrey holes 57
Australopithecines 17, 18, 19, 21, 22
Australopithecus afarensis 17
Australopithecus anamensis 18, 22
Australopithecus garhi 18, 22
Avebury 56, 57
Aztec 2, 7, 110, 111, 114, 115, 116, 117, 118, 122
Aztlan 114, 117

B

Babylonia 64, 66, 67
Badari 69, 70, 74
Ball game 104, 112, 117
Bands 8
Basal hominins 15, 16, 17, 21
Belas Knap 56
Beringia 37, 38, 41
Bering Land Bridge 35, 37, 40, 41
Bernardo de Sahagun 114
Bipedal 16, 17, 18
Bluefish Caves 37, 41
Bluestones 57
Bobongara Hill 34
Bradshaw paintings 35
Broad-Spectrum Revolution 51, 58
Broca's area 21, 22

C

Cactus Hill 36, 38, 41
Cahokia 103, 107
Capacocha 123
Çatalhöyük 53, 54, 59
Chaco Canyon 104, 105, 106, 108
Chan Chan 121, 124, 125
Chandragupta Maurya 96, 98
Charles Darwin 15, 22
Chauvet Cave 30, 32
Chavín de Huántar 119, 123, 124
Chetro Ketl 105
Chichen Itza 113, 115, 117
Chiefdoms 8, 13
Chimpanzees 1, 5, 16, 17, 21
Chimú 121, 124, 125
Chinampas 114
Cippi 81
Cishan 89, 90
City-states 2, 8, 13, 64, 69, 71, 74, 81, 87, 102, 106, 112, 115
Cleopatra VII 74, 75
Clovis first model 35
Colossal stone heads 110, 115
Context 12, 14
Coobool Creek 34, 41, 128
Copan 113, 117
Cordilleran 38, 41
Cotton 93, 94, 95, 119, 120, 122, 125
Cranial deformation 34, 121, 128
Cranial deformation 34
Cro-Magnon 28, 32
Cryptocrystalline 19
Cuauhtemoc 115, 118
Cultural relativism 7
Culture 5, 6, 7, 10, 13, 34, 35, 36, 38, 58, 64, 80
Culture change 7, 9, 10, 13
Culture history 9
Cuneiform 62, 64, 65
Cuzco 122, 123, 124, 125

D

Del Castillo 114

Demotic 71
Devil's Lair 34
Diffusion 7, 9, 13
Dogs 44, 45, 46, 47, 52, 54, 69, 70, 86, 99, 114
Dolmens 56, 57
Domestication 1, 9, 43, 44, 45, 46, 48, 49, 51, 52, 99, 128
Domestication 43, 46, 49
Dust Cave 46, 47, 99, 106

E

Early Arrival model 35, 41
Ecofacts 12
Edward B. Tylor 5
Egypt 1, 7, 45, 69, 70, 71, 73, 74, 75, 94
El Castillo 113, 115, 117
El Paraiso 119, 123, 124
Empires 8, 13, 66, 74, 89
Erlitou 86, 89, 90
Etowah Mounds 102
Etruscan civilization 2, 80, 81

F

Features 7, 11, 12, 86
Fertile Crescent 1, 51, 52, 58, 59
Flintknapping 9, 19
Florentine Codex 114, 118
Flotation 11, 14
Francisco Pizarro 123, 125

G

Gilgamesh 62, 67
Giza 71, 72
Goat's Hole Cave 29
Gorham's Cave 27
Great Bath 95, 96, 98
Great Sphinx 72
Great Wall 88, 89
Grotte XVI 25
Gwion Gwion 35, 41

H

Hammurabi Code 64, 66
Han 88, 91
Harappa 2, 94, 96, 97, 98
Harappan civilization 2, 93, 96, 98
Hayonim Terrace 52
Henge 56, 103
Hernán Cortés 115, 116, 118
Hierakonpolis 69, 70, 74
Hieratic 71
Hieroglyphics 70, 74, 75, 110
Hohokam 2, 104, 105, 106, 107, 108
Holism 6, 13
Homo erectus 19, 20, 21, 22, 23, 24, 25, 26, 27, 28, 33
Homo habilis 19, 21, 22
Homo neanderthalensis 24, 27, 31
Hopewell 101, 102, 106, 107
Hopewell Mound Group 101
Horizontal excavation 11
Huayna Capac 123
Huizilopochtli 114, 117
Hybridization 27, 32
Hypsithermal 100, 106

I

Ice Age 2, 23, 24, 25, 26, 27, 31, 33, 37, 38, 43, 44, 49, 51, 99, 106, 109, 123
Inca 2, 120, 121, 122, 123, 124, 125
Inca Trail 122
Indian Knoll 47, 100, 106
Indus Valley 2, 93, 94, 95, 96, 97, 98
Invention 7, 9, 13, 89, 91

J

Jane Goodall 5
Jerf el Ahmar 53
Jericho 52, 53, 58, 59
Jōmon 85, 86, 89, 90

K

Kebara 26, 32
Kebarans 51, 52, 58
Kennewick Man 38, 39, 42
King Agamemnon 80, 82
King Ashurnasirpal II 65, 67
King Hammurabi 64, 66, 67
King Minos 78
King Narmer 71, 74, 75
King Radamanthys 78
Knossos 78, 79, 81, 82
Koster 99, 106
Kurgans 47

L

La Chapelle-aux-Saints Cave 26
La Cotte de St. Brelade 25
Laetoli footprints 18
Lagar Velho 27, 32
Lake Mungo 34, 40
Lascaux Cave 6, 30, 32
Laurentide 38, 41
La Venta 110, 115, 116
Law of Superposition 12, 14
Levallois technique 24, 31
Linear A 79, 82
Linear B 79, 80, 81, 82
Lothal 2, 94, 96, 97, 98

M

Maadi 69, 70, 74
Machu Picchu 122, 124, 125
Malinche 115, 118
Manos 110
Maurya civilization 96, 97, 98
Maya 2, 8, 112, 113, 115
Meadowcroft Rockshelter 36, 41
Megafauna 39, 43
Megaliths 58
Mehrgarh 93, 97

Menhirs 56
Menhutep II 72, 75
Mesa Verde 105, 106
Mesopotamia 2, 61, 62, 63, 64, 65, 66, 67, 94
Metates 110
Mexica 114, 116, 117
Migration 7, 9, 13, 33, 40, 43
Minoans 2, 77, 78, 81
Mobile art 29
Moche 2, 120, 121, 123, 124, 125
Moctezuma II 115, 118
Mogollon 2, 104, 105, 106, 108
Mohenjo-daro 2, 94, 95, 96, 97, 98
Monk's Mound 103, 107
Monte Alban 110, 115, 116
Monte Verde 37, 38, 41
Mostly Out of Africa 27, 32
Mound 72 103, 107
Moundsville 102
Mousterian industry 24, 31
Multi-Regional model 27
Mycenae 80, 81, 82
Mycenaen civilization 2, 79, 80, 81, 82

N

Nahuatl 111, 115, 118
Naqada 69, 74
Narmer tablet 71, 75
Native American Graves Protection and Repatriation Act 39
Natufian 52, 53
Nauwalabila I 34, 40
Nazca 2, 120, 123, 124
Neanderthals 1, 21, 23, 24, 25, 26, 27, 28, 29, 31, 32, 33
Necropolis of Banditaccia 81, 83
Nefertari 72
Neolithic 52, 53, 54, 55, 56, 57, 58, 59, 77, 86, 90, 93, 97
Newark Earthworks 101
Nile 2, 8, 69, 71, 72, 74
Nimrud 65, 66, 67

O

Oldowan tool industry 19
Olmec 110, 111, 112, 115, 116
Oracle bones 87, 90
Orrorin tugenensis 17, 22
Ötzi 55, 56
Out of Africa model 27
Overkill Hypothesis 40

P

Pacific Coastal route 38
Palenque 113, 117
Paleoindian 39, 42, 99, 106, 109
Paranthropus 17, 18
Parietal art 30, 31
Past life ways 9
Pazyryk 47, 48, 49
Pedra Furada 37, 41
Pengtoushan 86, 89, 90
Phaistos 78, 79, 81, 82
Phaistos Disc 79
Pithoi 78
Potassium-argon dating 12
Poverty Point 100, 106, 107
Pre-Clovis model 35, 37, 41
Predmostí 29
Pre-Pottery Neolithic 53
Provenience 11, 14
Pueblo Bonito 105, 108
Pull Model 44, 49
Push Model 44, 49
Pyramid of the Moon 111
Pyramid of the Sun 111, 115, 116

Q

Qin 87, 88, 90, 91
Quechua 121, 123, 125
Quipu 122, 124, 125

R

Radiocarbon dating 12
Ramesses II 72, 73, 74, 75
Read 100, 106
Relative dating 12
Roonka 34, 41
Rosetta Stone 70, 74, 75, 79, 110

S

Sacsayhuaman 122
Sahelanthropus tchadensis 16, 17, 21, 22
Sahul 33, 34, 40
San Jose Mogote 109, 110, 115, 116
San Lorenzo 110, 115, 116
Sargon 63, 64, 65, 66
Sarsen 57
Seated Goddess 54
Seriation 12, 14
Shang 86, 87, 89, 90
Shangdi 87
Shanidar 1 25, 32
Shi Huang 2, 87, 88, 90
Siberian Ice Maiden 48, 49
Silk Road 88, 91
Sipan 120, 123, 124
Skara Brae 55, 59
Snaketown 104, 106, 107
Solutrean Hypothesis 38
Southeastern Ceremonial Complex 103, 104, 106, 107
Spirit Hill 47
Star Carr 54, 55, 59
Stonehenge 1, 57, 101
Sui 89
Sumerian civilization 2, 62
Sunda 33, 34, 40
Symbols 6, 67, 70, 71, 72, 73, 75, 79, 94
Systematic surveys 10

T

Tell 10, 21, 31, 38, 53, 65, 90

Templo Mayor 114, 117
Tenochtitlan 114, 115, 116, 117
Teosinte 109, 116
Teotihuacan 110, 111, 115, 116
Thebes 71, 72, 73, 75
Tikal 112, 113, 117
Tiwanaku 121, 123, 124
Tlaloc 114, 117
Tlateloco 114, 117
Toltecs 114, 117
Tomb of the Terra Cotta Soldiers 88
Tres Zapotes 110, 115, 116
Tribes 8, 13, 39, 104
Tula Grande 114, 116, 117
Tumuli 56
Tutankamun 73, 74, 75

U

Ur 62, 63, 66, 67
Uruk 2, 61, 62, 63, 64, 66, 67

V

Venus figurines 29, 31, 32
Venus of Willendorf 29
Vertical excavation 11

W

Wallacea 33, 38, 40
Wari 121, 123, 124
Washoe 6
West Kennet Long Barrow 56

X

Xia 86, 87, 89, 90
Xi'an 87

Y

Yinxu 87

Z

Zhou 86, 87, 90
Ziggurat 62, 63, 66

CPSIA information can be obtained at www.ICGtesting.com
Printed in the USA
BVOW10s1228200715

409536BV00001B/1/P